HAUNTED INNS

HAUNTED INNS
of
NORTHAMPTONSHIRE

Dorothy Priest

W. D. WHARTON
WELLINGBOROUGH

First published in 2007 by
W. D. Wharton
37 Sheep Street
Wellingborough
Northamptonshire NN8 1BX
Tel: 01933 222690

Dorothy Priest asserts her moral right to
be identified as the author of this work

ISBN-10 1-899597-21-2
ISBN-13 978-1899597-21-5

Typeset by John Hardaker
Wollaston, Northamptonshire

Printed and bound in Great Britain by
Impress Print, Corby, Northamptonshire

FOR
KATIE

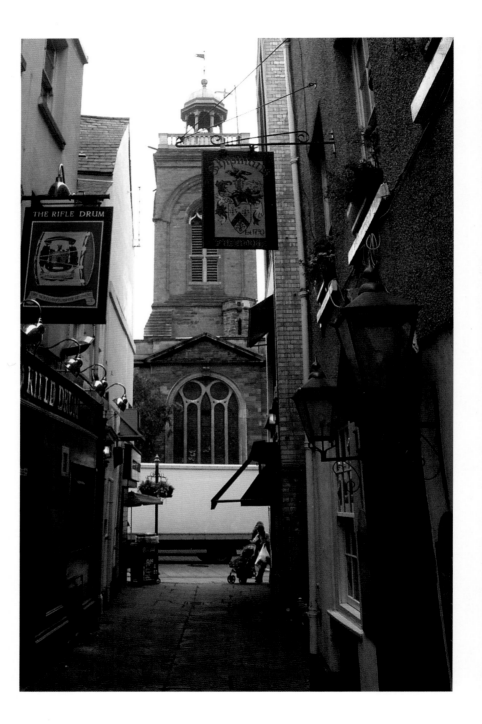

Contents

Preface

In Northamptonshire, as in other English counties, the village inn has always been at the centre of local community life and over the centuries these inns have performed functions no one would expect our modern pubs to take on. Some were used as courts where justice, legal or otherwise, would be meted out with the harsh punishments of the time taking place near at hand. Some have acted as mortuaries, while others have been the venue for a local wake with the coffin occupying a prominent position on the bar, and many times violent and unpleasant crimes have taken place in and around these buildings.

The Northamptonshire innkeeper has acted as judge and jury, banker, farrier and brewer and was plying his trade when our county town received its first charter from Richard the Lionheart and when Mary was executed at Fotheringhay. He was serving his brew when Charles Stuart fled Naseby field and when Earl Cardigan led that historic charge at Balaclava. No wonder they are the repository of so much of our colourful history.

Sadly there has been a great change in the brewing scene over the last century and inns are being demolished to make way for private housing or fast food outlets. Others have been sold to the brewers and given modern trendy names with decor to match while the long serving innkeeper has been replaced by a manager who holds the position for a year or two before moving on. In this way the old traditions and stories, once the innkeeper's stock in trade, are fast disappearing along with Northamptonshire's individuality and heritage.

As Hilaire Belloc said, the truth of the matter is ...

*"When you have lost your inns, drown your empty selves,
For you will have lost the last of England."*

Acknowledgements

I am indebted to those 'mine hosts' who welcomed me into their inns and patiently answered my questions about their experiences.

My gratitude is also due to the librarians at the *Chronicle and Echo* for allowing me access to their files, to staff at public libraries throughout Northamptonshire for their generous assistance and to those researchers who have gone before.

Special thanks go to Liz for her excellent company on our journeys around the county, and to Kevin for his patience and technical advice.

Indeed, to everybody who has had anything to do with the preparation of this book ...

Thank you!

Introduction

Of course many ghost stories may be the result of gossip, legend or superstition, but on my travels around the county I have met many sincere, intelligent people who have witnessed things to which they could put no explanation. From them have come these spooky, colourful and entertaining old tales which are based on fact, or the teller's interpretation of what is believed to be fact.

As to the truth of people's experiences, I try to keep an open mind, but the reality is that, over centuries, different people at different times have witnessed the same phenomena and have described them in exactly the same way. To pass this off as mere chance is perhaps stretching coincidence too far.

One explanation may be that an event, traumatic or otherwise, in some way imprints itself on its surroundings and is replayed, time after time, as the participants walk and behave as they once did in a time which no longer exists. Some seem aware of the modern-day viewer while others do not, and for that there is no answer. As I have been told on numerous occasions, "There's no logic to these hauntings!" But then, who said there had to be?

When reading these tales, please bear in mind that spirits dislike spending too much time on view. The average time for an apparition to reveal him or herself is apparently between five seconds and a minute. Any longer would be a world record.

MONTAGU ARMS
Barnwell

The Montagu Arms *derives its name from the family who were given the manor of Barnwell by Henry VIII after the dissolution of the monasteries. It is a traditional country inn and stands beside a tree-lined brook which runs down the centre of the village, passing thatched cottages of local stone, before eventually finding its way to the Nene. Three fords and a stone bridge cross the small brook and lead to the inn, parts of which date back to the 16th century.*

Barnwell was once a 'considerable town' possessing a castle, two parish churches, a weekly market, a fair and a regular visit from the circuit judge.

Even more important perhaps were the seven miraculous wells in the village, the waters of which were believed to cure any ailing infant. In time so many mothers flocked to them with babes in their arms that the church, alarmed at this 'heathen behaviour', banned the whole business as superstition. I wonder, after this, how many desperate mothers 'hedged their bets' and crept quietly to a well, their child hidden under their cloaks away from prying eyes.

The manor and castle of Barnwell lies just off the A605 to Oundle and remained in the Montagu family until just before the First World War when it was purchased by the Duke of Gloucester after his marriage to Lady Alice Montagu-Douglas-Scott, the daughter of the ninth Duke of Buccleuch.

Old Barnwell Castle.

The haunting, fairly well authenticated over the years, takes place outside the inn, and it is to an earlier family that the eerie happenings are linked. For within the gardens of the Manor House lie the ruins of a 13th-century castle which was founded by Berengarius le Moine, 1111-1163. Known as Berengar the Monk or 'Black Berengar' by the locals, the legend tells us that after quarrelling violently with his brother over a woman, he murdered him by walling him up somewhere in the castle.

Where this dastardly deed took place is open to conjecture, but the north-east tower of the castle is said to have a strange and frightening atmosphere and it was here on November 9th 1948 that two friends decided to hold a seance using a Ouija board. The story goes that as time went by the air became more and more oppressive until with a loud crack the upper half of a monk appeared, brandishing a whip. What became of the two young men is not recorded.

The *Montagu Arms* in Main Street in the 1930s.

Over the intervening years stories have been told by local villagers of a black-cloaked monk-like figure striding through the village, past the inn and the old cottages cracking his whip, terrifying all who see him. I am informed that in the late 1980s, in the vicinity of the inn, a young man walking his dog late at night was suddenly confronted by this terrifying spectre. The young man soon recovered but apparently his pet fled yelping into the night and took a lot of finding when daylight came.

The moss-covered stone said to cover the remains of Berengar the Monk.

It is said that the phantom is most often seen at the end of the village in the graveyard where the mausoleum of the Earls of Sandwich can be found. Interred there is the Earl of Sandwich whose name became a household word from the time when, rather than leave the gambling table to go and eat, he ordered meat between two slices of bread; also the notorious John, the 4th Earl, who died in 1792. A politician 'on the make', he was responsible for the rotten timbers used in the building of the great ship the *Royal George* which sank in 1782. Eight hundred men went down with her.

The mausoleum of the Earls of Sandwich in Barnwell graveyard.

However, standing near the entrance to this graveyard is an old flat tombstone said to be that of Berengar the Monk. Badly pitted and covered heavily in moss, it lies almost hidden in the surrounding grass. When the light is right it is just possible to make out the form of a figure on the stone. Standing in front of it as the sun goes down, I believe that I too would walk softly at this end of the village, listening carefully for the sound of a whip cracking just behind me.

THE ADMIRAL NELSON
Dark Lane, Braunston

Although the inn is named after the hero of the Battle of Trafalgar, fought in 1805, there is no record of any inn by that name in Braunston before 1830. However, great deeds demand remembrance and so it is with The Admiral Nelson, *named after one of England's greatest seamen.*

Dating from 1730, the inn stands at the blind end of Dark Lane in Little Braunston beside a lock on the Grand Union Canal and is haunted by two or more phantoms.

Seen by staff and guests alike, the first of the spirits is a woman in old-fashioned dress who moves quietly along the corridor towards the blocked up doorway which once went through to the adjoining Nelson's Cottage. Others speak of being accompanied by an unseen presence when using that part of the building and, although there is no clue to the lady's identity in the pub history, it is safe to assume that she once walked these floors in the flesh.

The Admiral Nelson in 1950.

The second is the spectre of an old chimney sweep, dubbed 'The Man in Black' who wanders the inn in a familiar fashion. The first recorded sightings of this gentleman took place in the late 1980s when Manns & Norwich Brewery in Northampton began an extensive refurbishment leading to structural changes to the bar. During this time customers, several of whom had never been in the inn before, reported seeing a ghostly presence and all described a man in period costume with a blackened face, a bit like a chimney sweep, with dirty clothes and a sooty appearance.

Since then the phantom has been seen to walk straight through a locked doorway to a chimney, blocked up many years ago. He also appears to show interest in the catering arrangements at *The Admiral Nelson* for not only has he been seen in the dining room at table No. 17, but on one occasion tried to attract the attention of the chef by placing a hand on his shoulder. At the time the member of staff was washing up in the kitchen and at the sound of breaking glass staff rushed in to find a very shaken young man and no one else.

The resident phantoms appear to move around quite confidently, for staff sometimes catch a glimpse of dark trousers or a skirt passing through a door and into the old cloakroom area. They say there is never a sound from the door catch which, when checked, is found to be working as well and as loudly as it always does.

The inn is also believed to have a resident poltergeist whose identity is unknown. Lively and mischievous, it not only rattles and moves all the glasses on the top shelf behind the bar but hurls beer mats into the laps of unsuspecting customers while pictures, securely hung, fall from their hooks.

However, the spirits, while active, are never unfriendly and *The Admiral Nelson* is a very pleasant canal-side pub, with good food and traditional cask-conditioned beer. In fact, it is the ideal place to sit on a warm summer's day to watch the pleasure boats on their journeys along the peaceful canal.

The Grand Union Canal on its way to Braunston.

THE GEORGE INN
Brixworth

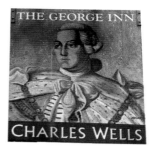

The George *is a 600-year-old coaching inn with a sign that probably denotes King George IV, one of the more popular monarchs. At one time the inn became an important coaching stage on the route between London and the North, its boast being that it had the fastest changeover of horses in the country. In fact such was the haste in changing the teams that the stone wall at the old front entry to the narrow inn yard has been worn on one side by horse flesh.*

The village of Brixworth is famous for its early Saxon Church of All Saints, but in Victorian times the Brixworth Board of Guardians became infamous as the 'Bury-all board'. This was a witticism on the name of the chairman, Canon W. Bury, the Rector of the village of Harlestone, who always referred the poor to the workhouse in order to keep down the rates rather than grant them outdoor relief. It was said that Brixworth was "the only union in the county where such a harsh and cruel system prevailed."

The village is the proud possessor of two ancient inns, but it is *The George*, dating back over six centuries, that has a history of supernatural activity. Standing on the crossroads in Brixworth, the inn has a good all round view, invaluable in a time of war. This obviously appealed to Cromwell, for it is said that on the eve of the Battle of Naseby, after locking the protesting landlord in his own cellar, he commandeered the inn, setting his men to maintain a watch from 'Cromwell's Eye'. This is the name that was given to a tiny window, still in existence today, which overlooks the courtyard and Newlands.

The story goes that, sometime during Cromwell's occupation, a 16-year-old boy, a runner for the general, was murdered in the stables of the inn. The how and why of this deed is not recorded but it is believed to be the spirit of this

unfortunate boy which, over the years, has been responsible for the odd happenings which take place at *The George*.

The first real indication of trouble comes from a letter written in 1698 by the estate manager, Gilbert Clarke, to his master Sir Thomas Isham, then in Italy. It reports that "2 Brixworth widows [staying at the inn] were tormented by such knocking at windows, and it lies as a heavy weight upon them sometimes, and sometimes rootes like a hogge in ye bedstraw, and twitches their head clothes." The bedroom that the ladies occupied is still there above the old coach entrance on the main road.

After that, little is heard for a long time about ghostly disturbances – at least until recently when a previous landlord and several of his customers reported regularly seeing strange faces in a walkway which once connected the inn to the cottage next door. Now, whether the patrons were entering or leaving the inn at the time of the sightings is a moot point, but there is certainly a sense of remoteness, even loneliness, in the tiny yard open to the sky, all that is left of the original passage.

The same landlord was often aware of an unseen presence in the bar – "I have twice opened up the bar and been serving to find that the gas bottles have been switched off. I'm always the last to leave at night and I haven't turned them off."

The present landlord has had his fair share of poltergeist activity, for on one occasion a large glass bowl full of candles for a children's cake jumped from its secure position on the table to land on the floor in pieces. Heavy doors swing open and closed of their own volition,

The room in which two Brixworth widows were 'tormented'.

and glasses fall off shelves while no one is near them.

An animal that is recognised as being extremely sensitive in the presence of the paranormal is the dog and the landlord's Golden Retriever is no exception, often staring and growling at nothing visible to the staff. The animal refuses to enter the inn cellar or even go through the nearby connecting door. Steak has been used to tempt him down there but without success, and if carried down he whines, struggles and scrambles to get away. No obvious explanation can be found for the animal's behaviour.

Although the blame for the hauntings is laid at the young 'runner's' door, an inn this old is bound to have some sinister episodes in its history which, over the centuries, have long been forgotten. However, apart from the faces on the walkway there is no record of any materialisation having taken place, so we will never know who really wanders *The George Inn*.

THE RED LION
Brixworth

This is the sign of John of Gaunt, fourth son of Edward III.

At one time *The Red Lion Inn* with its thatched roof and distinctive chimney stacks stood on a sharp bend on the Northampton Road in Brixworth. The bend, at that time, was so sharp that at the turn of the century long carts had to be manhandled or 'bump turned' to get them around the corner. Then in 1928 the old building was demolished and rebuilt back from the corner to its present site.

There appears to be only one spirit roaming this inn, a man who wanders the corridor behind the bar and who is seen or sensed in the kitchen area as well as in the bar. He has never been identified but one of the staff has been known to move automatically out of the way of this phantom as he goes past her, before realising that no one is to be seen.

The Red Lion before 1928. (Courtesy: *The Red Lion*)

The Red Lion, Brixworth, in the 1950s.

23

Another haunting only slightly connected to *The Red Lion* concerns an old-fashioned coach which, for two hundred years, has been seen on the Harborough Road just past the Boughton crossroads. One sighting took place about 8 p.m. one evening when a mother and daughter, driving in their car to the inn, saw what appeared to be a flickering light ahead of them. The nearer they got the more they realised that they were heading straight for the vehicle and the car driver braked sharply, only to pass straight through the vision.

Shocked and shaken they arrived at *The Red Lion* to be told by a Brixworth resident, "Most people know about it. It's been going on for 200 years."

FALCON HOTEL
Castle Ashby

This sign has always been one of importance in a county which for centuries has shown staunch allegiance to the reigning monarch. Associated with the royal sport of falconry, it was also part of the Yorkist crest during the Wars of the Roses and later a crest of Elizabeth I.

The building itself dates back to 1594 and was originally an Elizabethan farmhouse. By 1645 the sheds, still part of the present inn, belonged to the village blacksmith whose shade has wandered the inn for over 300 years.

Much of Northamptonshire's history is bound up with the Civil War and at that time one of Charles' most loyal subjects was the Marquess of Northampton whose family have owned Castle Ashby for over four centuries. The Earl raised his own regiment and he and his four sons all played a conspicuous part in the struggle, so it is not surprising that most on the estate were of the Earl's persuasion and not about to retreat before the enemy.

It was just before the Battle of Naseby that Cromwell's soldiers came to the little village of Castle Ashby. They were in an ugly mood for they had just spent a great deal of valuable time laying siege to and taking Compton Wynyates, the Warwickshire seat of the family. We are told that, dismounting on the green, they ordered the village blacksmith to shoe their mounts, which he refused to do, so without hesitation they hung him from the walnut tree in the garden of the inn.

Now, the staunch old royalist haunts the wine cellar and two of the bedrooms, especially the room which overlooks the old walnut tree. There is also a suggestion that he likes to relax with a pipe, for on one occasion an aroma of tobacco surprised the lone non-smoker in room No. 4.

Proprietor Neville Watson has been hearing about the spirit ever since he took over the *Falcon* in 2005 but is happy for the blacksmith to remain in residence for, although he is often heard by staff and customers, he appears to be a popular ghost. "He is a nice sort of chap and no one ever complains."

There is a further little tale, rather unpleasant, about a woman in the village, said to be the wife of the blacksmith and 'known' to be a witch. When she died, instead of cutting off her hands in order to prevent her casting spells after death, she was buried in the churchyard at Castle Ashby with her headstone facing away from the church towards the wall. Another way, apparently, of averting any power she might cast from the grave, although I find it odd that in the 17th century a witch would be put to rest in hallowed ground, for the custom was usually otherwise.

THE SPENCER ARMS
Chapel Brampton

The building dates back to 1637 when it was an ale house for estate workers and villagers and was known as The Stag's Head. *Then in 1824 it was renamed in honour of the owner, Earl Spencer of Althorp.*

Although over the centuries many odd events have taken place in the county's inns, perhaps one of the more bizarre which took place in this 17th-century inn was the holding of a wake with the coffin containing the deceased laid in the place of honour on the bar.

This, of course, happened years ago and so far there is no suggestion that the occupant of the coffin is still around in *The Spencer Arms.*

THE FOX AND HOUNDS
Charwelton

The Fox and Hounds is an attractive stone building, lying about 200 yards away from the famous packhorse bridge. The inn has plied its trade in the village for over two hundred years and has a name whose origin is of a sporting nature.

The little village of Charwelton is the birthplace of the River Cherwell which flows through Oxford to the Thames on its way to the sea. At one time the source of the river could be found in the cellar of old Cherwell Farm which once stood nearby on the Helidon road. Since the old house was demolished, the source of the Cherwell springs from a pool near the new farmhouse.

The village, with its attractive stone cottages, is famous for its ancient packhorse bridge which for 700 years carried travellers safely across the Cherwell. Fourteen feet long and just over one yard in width, it is now bypassed by the A361 Banbury to Daventry road which runs just alongside, taking all the heavy traffic.

This spooky encounter does not take place in the inn, but close by on the Banbury side of the packhorse bridge where, one spring evening, a motorist was horrified by the appearance of a man who suddenly appeared on the road in front of her. Without time to think she drove straight through him only to realise that there had been no impact of any kind and certainly no body lying in the road.

Although the driver was aware of the man looking straight at her as she drove towards him there was no face to be seen. His clothing appeared to be of an earlier time for, "He carried a great coat over one shoulder and carried either a pick or a gun," while over his head he wore "a brown sackcloth type of hood or cowl."

The figure has never been identified and certainly no one in *The Fox and Hounds*, where we made our enquiries, could give any explanation for the sighting.

However, in 1821 a notorious murder took place at old Cherwell Farm when a wealthy, elderly farmer was fatally injured by a shotgun blast which came from a nearby barn.

Before he died, the farmer, Mr Clarke, laid the guilt squarely at the door of his wife's lover, Philip Haynes. A hue and cry was immediately mounted but it was not until a week later that the suspect was found hiding in the barn from where the shot had been fired. With him was his gun.

The final 'proof' of his guilt was letters found in his room which had been written by Mrs Clarke inciting him to do away with her husband. Nothing more was needed and after a short trial they were both condemned to hang, which was carried out on Saturday March 10th, after which their bodies were 'disected and anatomized'.

Perhaps on that spring evening Philip Haynes, with his gun over one shoulder, re-trod the footpaths he knew so well in life … all good healthy speculation, no doubt.

THE BULL' S HEAD
Harborough Road
Clipston

Known to be a hard working animal, the bull has been used on many inn signs, especially in rural areas. This building dates back to 1627 and has, since that time, remained predominantly an inn, with antique oaken settles and high-backed chairs giving it a comfortable, traditional feel.

Over the centuries Clipston has been associated on three occasions, albeit it at a distance, with Royalty. The earliest was the nearby presence of a 'palace' or hunting lodge owned by King John and from where he would set forth to chase the local wildlife as a break from feuding with his unruly subjects.

Later, in the 14th century, Edward Prince of Wales took over the Lordship of the Manor of Clipston, while in 1645, after the Battle of Naseby, the King's coach fleeing the field was

stopped by the Parliamentarians in 'Clipston Field'. It is said that Cromwell's men mercilessly massacred the passengers, including the women, and confiscated a 'cabinet containing much of Charles' private correspondence.'

The Bull's Head inn stands on the Harborough Road out of Clipston and was a popular venue for young American pilots from Harrington Air Base. Known as 'The Carpet-baggers' they flew agents and supplies at night and in great secrecy to and from Occupied Europe. Some of those young men didn't return but their coins are where they left them, in the cracks of the centuries-old beams above the bar, placed there to pay for drinks if they returned or for a toast to them if they didn't.

Such a place must surely have a ghost; in fact it has at least two. The first is an unknown phantom dressed in long white robes which regularly appeared to a previous landlord near the window in the central area of the inn which looks out onto the Harborough Road.

Coins on the bar beams left by airmen during World War II.

So great an impression was made on 'mine host' that even twenty years after his retirement, when entering the inn for a drink, he would never sit in that particular area.

Another type of spectre, so far unseen, is said to wander the upper storey of *The Bull's Head* making children and animals aware of its presence. It appears that in 2004 the young daughter of the present landlord was found staring at a fixed point in her bedroom. What made it even more uncanny was the fact that both her pets, a cat and a dog, were standing immobile, staring at the same place. According to her father, the child became so frightened that she would stand and scream rather than enter that room, while her dog refused to go anywhere near it.

There have also been reports of odd happenings when the inn is closed for the night, for then heavy doors swing open and close of their own volition and chairs move across the floor without triggering the alarm.

Although no explanation is offered for these strange events, a report in the local paper of 1894 tells of an unexplained death which took place in the vicinity of the village. In the September of the previous year a 57-year-old general labourer, Bonsor Tarry, had arrived in Clipston and found himself both a job and a place to stay. Christmas came and went and on the evening of December 29th, after posting a letter, he was seen drinking in *The Bull's Head* and according to witnesses left there very cheerful and quite sober. He was never to be seen alive again.

As word of his disappearance got around searches were made of the area but without success. Bonsor Tarry was nowhere to be found. Weeks went by and then one day a shepherd passing a pond in a nearby field, on the route which Bonsor would have taken on his way home, saw the body of a man in the water. It was the missing labourer.

The verdict of the jury was 'accidentally drowned', for although the fence around the pond was broken there were no marks of violence on the extremely decomposed body and no one came forward with evidence of any kind. The quality of the original search was highly criticised, but the verdict had to stand.

Could it be that the shade of the drowned man returns occasionally to the place where he spent his last happy hours on earth, or is he looking for a revenge he can never take?

All is speculation!

THE RED LION
Clopton

The popularity of this sign was at its height between the fifteenth and seventeenth centuries, coming originally from the badge of John of Gaunt, 1340-1399, fourth son of King Edward III. In addition, when James I, the son of Mary Queen of Scots, ascended to the throne, he demanded that the red lion of Scotland be displayed on every public building, and by so doing show loyalty to the Crown.

Now a private house, this was once *The Red Lion.*

There has been an alehouse on the site at Clopton since the 12th century, but the present building, originally a coaching inn, dates from the 16th century and is now a private house, so please respect the occupants' privacy.

The old coaching inn and its environs have been haunted for centuries by a ghost known as Skulking Dudley. The story goes that in 1349 Dudley, then Lord of the Manor of Clopton, fought his cousin over the ownership of the estate. Feelings ran high for, by all accounts, it was a vicious fight with Dudley, the winner, mutilating and decapitating his cousin's body. His triumph, however, was worthless for it is said that, weighed down with guilt, Dudley became a shambling, stooping old man who died before his time.

Dead and buried perhaps but not gone, for over the years his ghost would be seen around the village, dodging in and out of hedgerows. His route took him from Clopton Manor through the yard of *The Red Lion* until he came to the small copse where the fight had taken place so many years before, known locally as Skulking Dudley Coppice. Unfortunately he didn't always stick to that route, for residents of the village would tell how his ghost walked the fields, entered houses, spooked the cattle and generally annoyed people.

Reported sightings of Dudley continued for over five hundred years but by 1905 the villagers were so fed up with the spectre wandering around the area, especially when they came late out of *The Red Lion*, that they asked for exorcism by the Bishop of Peterborough. The Bishop obliged and one night he and twenty-one clergymen, each carrying a lighted candle, walked the same route from the Manor moat to the coppice and back. After certain rites the candles were thrown into the moat and the ghost was laid to rest … or so it was believed!

However, as recently as 1994 Skulking Dudley was reported to be prowling the yew walk in the grounds of Clopton Manor as well as the lonely lanes between Clopton and Barnwell.

Apparently Skulking Dudley was not the last of his line, for it is recorded that Dudleys held the 'broad lands of Clopton' until 1764 when Sir William, last of the line, died in York. In the 1930s it was recorded that "all that remains in the way of records of the family is a pair of tablets, almost illegible, though on one of them can be deciphered the words '*Reliquiae ed Dudley*' …"

Clopton Manor, or Hall as it is now called, is probably a wing of the much larger building which was the seat of the Dudley family.

The old Yew Walk where Dudley is reputed to walk.

WOODEN WALLS
OF OLD ENGLAND
Collingtree

The meaning of this name and sign goes back to the great Athenian commander Themistocles, 525-406 BC who referred to the Greek fleet as "the wooden walls of Athens". Then, in 1635, in a speech to the judges, the phrase was coined by a Baron Coventry who stated that, "The wooden walls are the best walls of this kingdom".

Before the building of the M1, Collingtree was a quiet village of stone cottages and thatched roofs, but now the inn is the only thatched building left. The interior of the inn boasts timber beams constructed for ships of the 17th century and one of the beams, running right through the building, is said to be the longest continuous beam in the country.

Apparently, before the Battle of Naseby, the inn was patronised by Cromwell's soldiers who are said to have drunk

the inn dry. Adding insult to injury they refused to pay for their drinks and a brawl ensued in which some died.

Many years ago it was reported that one of the dead, a Roundhead officer, was buried nearby, from where he was often seen to walk to the inn, presumably in search of his long dead comrades. There have been no sightings for a long time now.

The *Wooden Walls of Old England* is a very pleasant village inn. You can be assured of a warm welcome and good food in pleasing surroundings.

THE KNIGHTS LODGE
Tower Hill Road, Corby

It is said that the inn got its name from a hunting lodge which once stood on this site. Later the building became a moated manor house and then a farmhouse before being converted into an inn in the early 17th century.

The original settlement of Corby goes back about 1000 years and began as a hamlet in the midst of Rockingham Forest. Indeed one of the earliest remains in the county was found there when, at the end of the 19th century, workmen excavating for ironstone uncovered a Bronze Age skeleton complete with half a dozen urns and a bronze dagger.

Now the good people of Corby were unhappy about leaving the old bones just lying there, and when the archaeologists arrived to study the find, the skeleton was missing, interred in a churchyard to find, one hopes, eternal peace.

Possibly the oldest building in the town, *The Knights Lodge* is a Grade II listed building and still retains a trapdoor in the floor leading down to ancient tunnels (presumably now collapsed) believed to run all the way to Rockingham Castle. Their actual destination and use is now lost in the mists of time but it is worth bearing in mind that it is all of two or three miles to the castle – a great feat of tunnel engineering for that time, if indeed they did exist.

As to the inn itself there appears little doubt that *The Knights Lodge* is haunted by spirits both visible and noisy. In an upstairs room a woman can sometimes be heard, weeping for her child, while the previous managers of the inn would often hear footsteps on the wide 17th-century staircase and the rustling of skirts as well as the sound of giggling and whispering in empty rooms.

However, there is more to the inn than unexplained noises, for a monk-like figure has been seen to glide across the floor, fading into the panelling opposite, en route to his destination.

A previous landlady who saw the spirit late one night after locking up watched in horror while her Cairn Terrier yapped and growled at the place where the figure had disappeared. She was to see it several times after that, always in the same place and always dressed in monk-like robes.

The present landlord, Mr Hope, admits to the building having an eerie feeling about it, especially when he comes down in the mornings, and particularly during the last eighteen months after he had awoken in the night to see a black, voluminous shape floating above him. The face was hidden, and as he sat up the spectre moved like lightning around the room before disappearing through the far wall, presumably out into the night, leaving the landlord wide awake and in a cold sweat. It was a long time before he fell asleep again that night.

An event not quite so frightening if no less mystifying is the awareness of something passing the office window when Mr Hope is at his desk. Not something to be thought of as unusual until you realise that the office is on the first floor.

Whatever roams the inn affects the landlord's pet Labrador for very often the animal will go berserk as it stands on the stairs looking down into the pub at something or someone invisible to human eyes.

The main area of disturbance appears to be around the old fireplace at one end of the inn where a drop in temperature often persuades a customer to don a coat, regardless of the warmth of the bar. However, this sudden chill does not appear to

The fireplace where a monk-like figure has been seen.

deter whatever stalks the inn, for quite recently, in broad daylight, Mr Hope was horrified to see a male figure in white drapes with some kind of hat or helmet on his head disappear through the wall. The sighting was over in a matter of seconds, leaving the landlord appalled and white faced.

On the second floor of the inn, under the roof of Collyweston slates, there is something neither seen nor heard but definitely sensed. The area is used only for storage but the atmosphere is so unpleasant that the landlord on entering admits that he "doesn't want to be there". The man who comes to repair the boiler on that floor is of the same opinion and makes his feelings very obvious.

One fact which might have a bearing on some of the supernatural events is that in the 12th century this site was in the possession of the Cistercian monks from Pipewell Abbey who later returned the land to the Crown in exchange for 'Giddington Church'.

In spite of these nocturnal visitors the inn is comfortable and traditional in its hospitality and well worth a visit.

THE HUNTING LODGE
High Street, Cottingham

The ancient settlement of Cottingham existed when Rockingham Forest stretched north to Stamford, and from Market Harborough across to Wansford. So the name of the inn is most appropriate in a village which once stood deep in the hunting preserves of the Norman Kings.

The present Hunting Lodge is a friendly, modern building with no trace of any apparitions, so far. It is the old Hunting Lodge restaurant, the original stable block of 18th-century Bury House, which is said to be haunted by two ghosts.

Although some say that the spirits are those of a former butler and a servant girl, the real perpetrator of the deed was in fact Sir Thomas Medlicott, an erstwhile Lord of the Manor in the mid-18th century. A most unpleasant man by all accounts, for after taking his wife Sarah to the attic high in the house, he pushed her from a window which overlooked the stables and watched while she fell to her death.

Although no one to my knowledge has ever seen a re-enactment of that foul deed, the spirits have lingered on down the years – whether in hate, revenge or curiosity, who can say?

The original stable block of Bury House.

41

However, it is told that at midnight on the 12th of every month Thomas, dressed all in black, stalks the area around Bury House. A local man working in the grounds of *The Hunting Lodge* said there are still people in the surrounding villages who will not walk or drive their cars down that stretch of road at that time.

As well as Thomas there are other spirits who wander the buildings but it's not known if they are connected to the original haunting. From time to time they show themselves. In the 1950s a young woman working there saw a face at the attic window. She ran up the stairs only to find the room empty, and she was adamant that no one could have passed her.

In 1971 an electrician working in that part of the building saw two figures in old-fashioned clothing walk along a corridor and disappear in front of him. Some years later the old restaurant cloakroom became known for its unfriendly atmosphere and strange noises which eventually became so unpleasant that regular customers wouldn't visit it alone.

Now, with the refurbishment of the old stable block, the spirits seem to have forsaken that part of their haunt. Perhaps the change is too great – that is until the twelfth of the month!

There is another more friendly haunting in the village. If you are a lone traveller on the old Corby Road in Cottingham late at night, you might suddenly become aware of a spectral animal in the shape of a black dog trotting along beside you.

This is nothing to be alarmed about, for the spectre, known as Shagfold, Shuck or Padfoot, often appears at night on this stretch of highway. It acts as a guardian, trotting close and seeming anxious to protect the traveller, but beware, for if touched the animal disappears along with its protection.

Nowadays, most people travel by car down that stretch of road and sightings of the spectre are rare.

The Hunting Lodge lies on a ridge of the Welland Valley in Northamptonshire, overlooking Rockingham Castle.

THE WHEATSHEAF
Daventry

The Wheatsheaf is a popular inn sign. It was once seen regularly on bakers' shops and it has been said that some inns sporting this sign also baked on the premises, combining two businesses in one. The inn has been in existence since 1610 but is now a home for the elderly.

The Wheatsheaf Hotel in the 1940s.

The ghost said to haunt this inn is Viscount Stafford, one time advisor to King Charles I. Arraigned for treason for allegedly suggesting that an Irish army should invade England and help put down the rebels, he was executed in 1640. The King, unable to save his friend, signed the death warrant and watched him walk to the block, unaware that they were destined to meet again five years later in rather unusual circumstances.

In 1645, Charles I came to Daventry with an army of 5,000 foot and horsemen with the intention of defeating Cromwell's Modern Army in Northamptonshire. However, while lodging at *The Wheatsheaf*, he was rather upset to be woken three times by the apparition of Stafford, who told him each time to move his army northwards and not to fight the battle near Daventry as he could never win the day. After each visit the

The Wheatsheaf Hotel, **now converted into a home for the elderly.**

King informed his military advisors of the warnings but was persuaded by Prince Rupert and others to ignore Stafford and remain where he was.

We are told that on the third night the spectre gave him a final warning, "Your cause is blighted beyond retrieve, if you but another day tarry here." Again no one believed him and the consequences were fatal, for on 14th June the disastrous Battle of Naseby was fought and the King's troops were routed.

Over 4,000 were reported dead on the battlefield, mostly on Dust Hill, and it is said that every 14th June, for the next hundred years, "Villagers would gather and sit overlooking the Hill and look up at noon and see and hear the battle fought out in the sky complete with regiments, horses and artillery."

> "Yearly on the field of Naseby,
> In the fragrant month of June,
> Silent as the stars that glimmer
> When the night is at its noon,
> Hosts of Warriors rise and muster
> 'Neath the shadows of the moon."

From 'The Battle of Naseby' in
Historical Legends of Northamptonshire, Alfred Story 1883.

Since then *The Wheatsheaf* has been modernised many times, with the bedroom where Charles saw Stafford being divided into two, and not until 1968 was the apparition seen again.

In that year a lady visiting the inn was awakened in the night by a ghostly figure which moved from one corner of the room to the door. The following night this intrepid lady decided to stay awake and keep watch, telling others later, "I suddenly felt extremely cold and saw a figure sitting on the bed in a drooping position, but as I watched it suddenly vanished."

That seems to be the last recorded incident of supernatural phenomena being witnessed at *The Wheatsheaf* but a strange presence and a distinct chill has often been felt in the divided rooms between the 6th and 26th of June.

THE COCK
Denford

The cock appears on many inn signs for it is easy to recognise and has at least three explanations. For centuries the sign has represented a place where food was available, while secondly 'cock' is the old word for spigot or tap referring to both bottled beer as well as draught ale. However, the stance and body of the bird on this sign leads us to a third explanation, the ancient sport of 'cock fighting', which often happened in and around inns. Take your pick.

As with many of our ancient Northamptonshire villages, Denford, 'the ford in the valley', was listed in the Domesday Book. Once a village of importance possessing two working mills, it is now a small rural community, tucked away just off the busy A45 between Ringstead and Thrapston.

The Cock, surrounded by 17th-century ivy-covered cottages, stands near the river on the old Northampton to Peterborough mail coach run. In front of it lies the smallest village green in the county, where you can sit at your ease with a drink and watch the world go by. The date on the building is 1593 and an old priest hole in the ceiling reminds you of the periods of religious persecution in the 16th and 17th centuries.

For hundreds of years the blacksmith, the most important of the village craftsmen, plied his trade next to the inn. Doubtless after a day spent working hard at the forge it was a relief to lay down his tools and go next door for a relaxing gossip along with much needed refreshment.

However, like many other craftsmen, the village black-smith's business fell in the face of the rise of the motor age, and the smithy, once an integral part of village life, is now part of *The Cock*. In fact it could be said that in spirit the old artisan has moved even closer, for his forge is now the bar area of the

pub and it appears he can't keep away; regulars have reported seeing an apparition of a blacksmith near the cloakroom, presumably dressed in his working garb for recognition.

One who came face to face with him in the cloakroom area hurried back to the bar 'as white as a sheet' and it was some time before he could describe his sighting to others.

The inn appears to boast two other restless spirits, one a poltergeist with a liking for kitchen equipment which goes missing for twenty-four hours before being returned to its original position, while the third spirit, an unidentified lady dressed in white, has reputedly appeared to customers on their way to and from the ladies' toilets. This female phantom is also blamed when the cubicle doors are found locked on the inside without being occupied. A spectre with a sense of humour!

The old brick fireplace with its supporting wooden beam and the bar area, which now stands where the old smithy used to be, helps the inn to retain its traditional atmosphere. It is a friendly country pub and restaurant in picturesque surroundings and sells six real ales and three types of beer.

THE WORLD'S END
Ecton

Local legend tells us that in the mid-18th century it was William Hogarth, a regular visitor to Ecton, who gave the inn its new name and painted the first signboard before presenting it to the landlord in recognition of his skill as a brewer of 'ye wholesome toddy'. The landlord was said to be very proud of the sign and took it in every night before locking up. Then one night he forgot and came down next morning to find that it had disappeared, never to be returned.

It is worth noting that in Hogarth's last engraving entitled 'Finis' where everything is lying in ruins, he drew a broken inn sign with the name 'The World's End'. The picture shows the globe bursting into a holocaust of flames. He hadn't forgotten.

First mentioned in 1678, the old coaching inn once known as the Globe lies in the small village of Ecton on the A4500 between Wellingborough and Northampton. It stands on a large triangle of land which in maps and tithe books has, for hundreds of years, been known as The World's End. Tradition tells us that it got its name from the time when it was used as a temporary prison compound for prisoners captured at the Battle of Naseby in 1645; a stopping place for the columns of prisoners who were herded along the dusty roads on their way to face trial in London. Many could go no further and died of their wounds or of the ill treatment they received from their captors. For them it was the world's end.

At that time the inn was used as a temporary prison hospital with the cellar as a mortuary, and over the years many landlords have reported disembodied footfalls and shadowy figures in the cellar. In 2002 a gas man, working on his own down there, saw a man from the knees up only walk straight in front of him across the cellar floor. Presumably the spectre

The World's End on the Wellingborough to Northampton Road.

was walking on a floor level of earlier times, as it is clear to see that the floor was at one time set much lower than it is now.

Over the years the old inn has been the scene of many reported manifestations. A little girl from Victorian times has been seen and heard in the attic flat; it is said that she died from diphtheria all those years ago. Then in 1995 a visitor was horrified when he handed a bowl to an old lady in the bar who then ... just disappeared. A possible connection to this phantom is a beam in one of the bedrooms where an old lady is said to have hanged herself over 100 years ago.

This old coaching inn has also been the scene of a classic haunting, for the ghost has the appearance and dress of a nun but the face is a fleshless skull. In 2002 she frightened a group of customers by appearing amongst them for a few seconds and then vanishing. They were able to describe her later as a woman wearing a long grey dress and visible to them as 'through a murky glass'.

The phantom nun is not, however, confined to the inn for it is said that at midnight every year on October 31st she appears on the road near where the gallows used to stand and stops anyone attempting to pass. The legend goes that in the 18th century, just before midnight, a coachman driving to Wellingborough from Northampton saw a figure standing motionless in the middle of the road. The horses were sharply pulled up as he shouted and cursed but to no avail, and jumping down to try other means of 'persuasion' he was horrified to see amidst the draperies a fleshless skull where the face should have been.

Scrambling back onto his seat, much faster than he got down, he tried to set the horses in motion but they refused to go forward. Eventually he managed to turn them and made his way to Wellingborough by a circular route.

The World's End
in front of the triangular green and the old toll road.

For hundreds of years, the front of *The World's End* faced south, overlooking the triangle of green around which the old toll road used to run. Then in the middle of the 18th century new barns and stables were added and the frontage changed to face north and the now A4500. Perhaps the spectral nun could be forgiven for not being aware of the change but the same could not be said of some amateur ghost hunters of recent fame. Determined to meet the nun, some young men, armed with deckchairs and refreshment to keep out the night chill, settled themselves at the crossroads on the A4500 just before midnight on October 31st. Whether or not the phantom appeared on the old road is not known but the intrepid ghost hunters waited in vain.

A rather spooky tale was recorded in the 1920s about a brother and sister who, returning from a feast at Mears Ashby in the late 1800s, saw a terrified woman stumbling towards them. She had seen a 'ghost' and took little persuasion to walk on with the young couple. Nervously and with many a glance behind they made their way homewards, only to be joined near Ecton Brook by a 'woman in grey', a stranger to them all. She regarded them in silence while they in turn stared in horror for they could see right through her. Seconds later she vanished.

There is no further record of the brother and sister. It is known only that the victim who saw her first was to die two weeks later.

It is interesting to note that Ecton Hall, now private housing and once the home of Sir John Brown, First World War hero and founder of the Territorial Army, was built on the site of an old nunnery and in the grounds there is still an area known as the 'nun's walk'.

A late 17th-century episode at the inn has had repercussions as recently as the 1990s. The episode concerned the then owner's niece, an attractive young woman called Angela who was being courted by a local lad named John. However, his affection was not returned for the girl was very much in love with a young Portuguese called Johan and was expecting his baby. Finding out about the relationship, John confronted his rival in the cellar and in a fit of despair killed both him and Angela before committing suicide. We are told that Angela's uncle, an unpleasant man, fearing either retribution or a loss in takings, then disposed of the bodies hoping that the news of these terrible events would never get out.

Of course he wasn't able to keep the tragedy secret and it is said that Johan and Angela still wander the inn searching for each other in vain, and over the years the sighting of a shadowy figure has been reported by staff and visitors alike.

The apparition certainly affected one young man who, in 1991, working behind the bar installing a CCTV camera, turned to see an indistinct figure looking straight at him. He was so unnerved that he found himself unable to move and what made it more frightening was the way in which the other workmen walked through the phantom, obviously unaware of it. The sighting lasted only a short while but I am told that the work behind the bar was finished in record time.

The most recent report came to me from a customer at the inn who, seated against the wall in the restaurant, felt a gentle but definite push on her arm. There was no one behind her and her position against the wall precluded any human contact from the side.

So there you have it, a myriad of ghosts, from the spectral nun who wanders the highways and byways of Ecton to the phantom in the cellar walking on a different plane to the rest of us. But don't let them alarm you for they are mostly harmless and the inn is comfortable and friendly. You are sure to enjoy your meal.

The World's End, Ecton, *c.*1920.

THE BELL
Bell Hill, Finedon

This name and sign originated on inns which stood close to a church and just up the hill from The Bell *stands the lovely old church of St Mary the Virgin. In medieval times it was believed that the sound of the church bell would not only protect the listener from storms and lightning but would also guard the souls of the dying from the powers of evil who would be waiting to take them. A comfort, perhaps, to regulars of the inn as they wended their ways home on dark and stormy nights.*

Set amongst the warm ironstone buildings of old Finedon *The Bell* is said to be the county's oldest hostelry, and Thomas Burke, in his book *The English Inn*, places it as the third oldest in England with a date of 1042. It is believed that Edith, the widow of Edward the Confessor, gave *The Bell* its licence in that year, and certainly in the Domesday Book of 1086 Finedon is recorded as long being in the ownership of the queen.

Centuries later came the railways and as the need for wayside inns declined the building became, once again, an ordinary farmhouse, only to be converted back to a recognised inn in 1872 by William Mackworth Dolben, the local squire.

Since many old farmhouses also traded as inns, it is possible that refreshment had always been available here. Certainly, before the present road was built, the original building faced onto the old road bordering the fields, while the side entrance which leads to the present car park was a narrow lane.

The building is ancient indeed and rumoured to be the haunt of the spirit of an outcast monk. This ghost is said to stalk the passages which link the inn to the church and, although the entrance to them has never been found, it is believed to begin in a cellar which lies somewhere beneath the inn.

Whether this haunting has any connection to the Monk's Cell over the south porch of the church is unknown. It is recorded that the cell was used originally by priests who were paid a pension of seven marks to sing Mass in the church and that one of these priests was buried in the churchyard in 1546. That he died a man of property and in holy orders there can be little doubt for he bequeathed to the church "a redd daffed cowe, a black pyed heefore and a blacke daffed cowe bullock".

Now whether *The Bell* harbours more than one spirit is open to conjecture but so many peculiar things have happened over the years that the possibility cannot be ignored.

On one occasion the two doors leading from the side of the inn to the bar swung silently open and then closed of their own accord to the amazement of the present owner who admitted that he felt the hairs on the back of his neck rise. No one had entered or left the inn, there was no wind and in any case the doors are heavy with strong latches.

The sound of footsteps have been heard in the inn coming from what is now the main entrance and continuing along a passageway, long blocked off, while at night the footsteps travel, sometimes quite loudly, along the landing of the inn which leads only to bedrooms. When checked the area is always empty.

There is also a cellar door in the inn with a mind of its own, for sometimes it refuses to open when needed, only to swing wide of its own accord minutes later after the member of staff has walked away.

Even customers are not immune to the spirit's activity. One reported feeling a hand touch him on the shoulder as though asking for attention but on turning round discovered that there was no one there.

The old fireplace with the stone likeness of Queen Edith's face set in the surrounds.

One of the few times a visual sighting has been reported was when a family member noticed a disembodied face staring at her through a window which looks out onto the courtyard at the back of the inn. Pressed against the glass, its features appeared soft and jelly-like and certainly unrecognisable as human and the lady admits to being terrified. A few days later a customer's dog, which normally roamed at will while his master was at the bar, refused to go anywhere near the area where the face had been seen.

Unexplained disturbances appear to go back a long way for I am told that in the mid-1950s the owner of *The Bell* 'lasted only a short time' as he was unable to cope with the odd happenings which were taking place there, such as doors which suddenly shut in his face when the inn was empty and closed.

The present owner has no such problem for he has been in residence for thirty-six years ... obviously a popular man with the spirits which roam *The Bell*.

TUDOR GATE HOTEL
High Street, Finedon

The Tudor Gate *began life as a 17th century farmhouse and was converted to an inn about 1720 when it was known as The Gate. Tudor was added more recently as an acknowledgement of the building's beginnings. At one time a bakehouse stood next door, joined to the inn by a courtyard but now the two buildings are one and the courtyard has been converted into a comfortable entrance hall.*

The *Tudor Gate* is said to possess two or more benevolent spooks whose activities appear to go back a long way.

A previous owner admitted that when he moved to the inn in 1967 he heard rumours of an indefinable presence lurking in the building. Then he began to hear disembodied footsteps and the sound of heavy breathing close at hand while doors opened and closed on their own – events for which no rational explanation could be found.

At that time reports were made of a lady who would sometimes be seen to walk the corridors, travelling through doors which would open and close behind her. Another story is told of a young man (a waiter) who, rather than go home late, would sleep over in room 11. However, this all changed after he woke up in the middle of one night to find an old lady sitting on the end of his bed. His reactions are not recorded but he never stayed the night again!

Then in 1981, renovations were put in hand and it was noticed that the manifestations ceased ... but not for long, for in 1993 the old bakery became a part of the inn and reports began of noises heard in empty rooms. These were all at the top of the building, once the living area of the old lady who had owned the bakery.

That same year a decorator who had worked at the inn many times before was there, late one night, finishing off a job. It was about 1.30 a.m. when something touched the side of his leg. Although aware of suddenly feeling cold he thought no more about it until ten minutes later when it happened again. This time he turned quickly around but there was no one to be seen and just as suddenly as it had dropped, the temperature rose again.

Disturbances at the inn have certainly not faded over the years, for odd happenings reported by customers and staff have continued right up to the present day.

Dogs bark frantically at an unseen presence in the reception area, chairs move around the rooms and a lady dressed in an old-fashioned pink dress has been seen to look out of a front window and wander around the Hartley Suite, although perhaps she has now moved on, for the last sighting of this 'bubbly blonde type' was twelve months ago.

The present manager is aware that the inn houses extra 'guests' for there are times when working at the main desk he senses someone walking up the ramp from the old courtyard, now the sitting area. Turning to welcome them he finds the area empty.

One other part of the building is said to have an uncanny atmosphere and that is the Orchard Suite which is separate from the main building. Used solely as a function room, members of staff will enter it only in pairs.

One of the spirits is said to be that of the old lady who owned the bakery so many years ago but for the rest ... no explanation has so far been found.

High Street Finedon, showing the cedar tree which was for many years a landmark outside the hotel.

THE OLD CHERRY TREE
Great Houghton

Built in 1576 by G. Robyns this is one of the oldest public houses in the county and certainly one of the most attractive. Its name and sign relate to when the eastern end of the town was famous for its cherry trees. Sadly those days are long gone but at least some of the fruit trees still line the lane where The Old Cherry Tree *stands.*

The ancient village of Great Houghton, standing on the southern slopes of the Nene valley was near to becoming a 'lost' village when, in the early 17th century, Francis Tresham, wanting to enclose the land for his own gain, was forced to change his mind when told, "you could not remove all the tennantes without much clamour and especiallie when itt is so neare to Northampton, whose affectiones are well knowen to you". Although down the centuries the village has retained its traditional identity, it has recently been incorporated into the Borough of Northampton ... it is to be hoped that the Borough does not succeed where Tresham failed.

From the records of supernatural activity at *The Old Cherry Tree* inn, which go back at least to the early 1940s, it appears that past inhabitants are reluctant to leave and who could blame them?

The sound of a lady singing and children running around in an upstairs room have been heard over the years. Indeed a previous landlady, while standing at the sink pumping water from the underground well, would hear quite clearly the sounds coming down a now-blocked-in staircase.

Another lady, young and dressed in the style of an earlier age with a white shirt and black skirt, has made herself known at least twice. The first time was in the doorway of the inn when she appeared to be waiting for someone. When spoken to by the then landlord, Mr Stevenson, she disappeared. However, this was not the end of their acquaintance, for she would also appear at the far end of the inn, once a cottage, smile at him and vanish. Whether this lady was ever connected to that next door cottage there is no way of knowing.

It also appears that the inn was at one time haunted by a 'gathering' of phantoms who 'made merry' in the cellar below the bar. This odd happening took place just after the war when the closing time for inns in the Borough of Northampton was 10 p.m. while just outside, for some reason, it was 10.30 p.m. Naturally at 10 p.m. everyone would dash over the border line to a more accommodating inn, one of which was *The Old Cherry Tree*, where the landlord was also happy to continue serving after hours, but discreetly in the cellar.

Then late one night the landlord's son came in to see a light under the stable door leading to the cellar and heard the sound of voices, but rather than join his father and his guests he decided to read the paper and have a quiet drink. Some time later, on going to wish the revellers a good night before making his way upstairs, he was rather startled to find the cellar dark

and empty and his parents asleep in bed, where they had been for some time. I leave the speculation to you!

Mr Bob Stevenson, who took over the inn from his parents in 1980, told me of a strange event which took place when he was a young man and at one o'clock every morning the sound of footsteps would be heard walking on the gravel down the side of the inn. At first these noises were dismissed as a nuisance but the footsteps came so often that it began to unsettle the landlord and his wife for, although watch was kept from inside the building, no one was ever seen. At last it was decided that a watch should be kept outside and one night Bob and a friend waited hidden at the far end of the courtyard. The footsteps began, but search as they might, they could find no one walking down the side of the inn or indeed anywhere else. After that night they were never heard again; it seems the nocturnal wanderer had decided to move on.

Over the years changes have been made in the inn. Fireplaces have been opened up, the old staircase has been blocked off and the spirits appear to have quietened down. Quietened down, yes, but not gone completely, for sometimes a presence is still sensed in the upstairs rooms where once a lady sang and children played and I have been told that, just occasionally, the sound of her singing can be heard, coming down a staircase that is no longer there.

The food and service at *The Old Cherry Tree* is excellent and the surroundings traditional and comfortable, and if it retains its phantoms from yesteryear they don't bother the customers. Why should they?

TOLLEMACHE ARMS
Harrington

This mid-16th-century inn takes its name and arms from the Tollemaches, the family of the Earls of Dysart. The 14th-century church lies some way away from the village and here, after the Battle of Naseby, the slain were laid to rest in the churchyard.

Since the time of Henry VIII, the *Tollemache Arms* has stood in the Saxon village of Harrington. The medieval manor of the village was owned by the Knights of the Order of St John of Jerusalem, passing into the hands of Sir John Stanhope during the reign of James I.

Around 1832 a member of the Stanhope family, one Reverend Hugh Tollemache, became rector of Harrington. Obviously well liked, the inn was renamed after this gentleman who was the incumbent of the parish for sixty years.

However, his replacement was of a different breed; for the Victorian Reverend Atkins, incensed with the locals who preferred the inn to the church on a Sunday, bought the Tollemache Arms and installed his coachman as landlord, thus

ensuring it would be closed on a Sunday. Not content with curbing his parishioners' drinking habits, he used that part of the inn which is now the restaurant as a mortuary for the village dead.

As far as I'm aware the *Tollemache Arms* has no history of a haunting but the inn overlooks the fields stretching away down the hill where the distraught spirit of Lady Jane Stanhope is said to roam.

The fields are all that is left of the elaborate gardens belonging to the Stanhope mansion which was demolished in the mid-18th century, and it was in this forgotten place that a gardener was beaten to death by Lady Jane. Apparently a minor mistake in the care of the garden led to the cruel and vindictive girl hitting him over the head with a shovel until he died.

Remorse overcame her too late, and for the rest of her life she walked, wringing her hands in grief, mourning over the old man and her terrible crime.

Although one would assume the spirit wandering the fields to be that of the old man cruelly done to death, it is Lady Jane who walks in the long dead garden known as 'Falls Field', dressed in white flowing robes, but beware, for as the legend tells us, anyone who sees her will shortly pine away and die.

A Victorian version of the haunting tells of a doctor and his daughter passing through the village near to 'Falls Field' where the little girl was adamant that she could see a lady in white walking slowly through the grass. The father could see nothing but, aware of the legend, he rushed his daughter home where she soon became ill and, although he devoted all his medical skills trying to save her, she slowly weakened and died.

THE GRIFFIN
Higham Ferrers

Although the sign on The Griffin *is an unusual one, it has always been a popular emblem, for it combines the head and wings of the eagle, thought of as the king of the birds, and the body of the lion, the king of the beasts.*

The Griffin stands on the High Street not far from the ancient market cross and the medieval church of St Mary's. Dating from the 17th century, the inn has had its fair share of odd disturbances, for it boasts one, if not two, unquiet spirits. The first, according to previous landlords, is an unidentified ghost whose heavy footsteps could be heard about the inn while lights would be switched off and on. Through all this the culprit remained invisible, though not unfelt, for on one occasion the lights went and the landlady felt herself being pushed gently down the stairs. Luckily she came to no harm!

The stone inglenook where the ghost of a young girl has been seen.

Further unexplained happenings took place when the following landlord and his wife took over in 1986. They found that items would go missing, some for long periods of time, while objects, including video tapes, were seen to fly off the top of the television. Sometimes they would be woken by incredibly loud music from a tape player used only for background music, which had been switched off for the night.

The hauntings continued when the present landlord and lady took over in 1991, bringing with them their two Red Setters, and it soon became noticeable that the dogs would refuse to enter certain rooms, barking aggressively at something or someone only they could see. Meanwhile poltergeist activity continued with lights blinking and objects disappearing only to reappear much later.

The Griffin Inn, Higham Ferrers, *c.*1960

Reports of another spirit stretch back much further. This disembodied ghost has been seen by several customers over the years, but only the bottom half of pantaloons and buckled shoes. Its favourite location appears to be a chair in the old stone inglenook and, although the spirit has always been thought of as male, it appears to have got the message across to some of the female customers that it is a young girl who suffered at the hands of Cromwell's soldiers.

If the ghost was indeed female, were the pantaloons donned as protection against the 'rough soldiery' frequenting the inn? If so they failed her. Be that as it may, the old coaching inn with its leather seating and open fireplaces has a warm welcome for the traveller. A pleasant pub and you will enjoy your meal.

MONK & MINSTREL
Isham

In 1779 this was the dwelling place of a Mr James Reynolds and the meeting place for the Society of Friends. The Quakers at that time were not a popular sect and their position just across the road from the beautiful 12th-century church must have seemed highly contentious to some of the regular members of St Peters Church. Early in the nineteenth century the private house was converted into an inn named The Red Lion. It now answers to the name of the Monk & Minstrel.

According to reports this inn, whose ironstone frontage has changed very little over the years, has been for some time the scene of supernatural occurrences. It appears to boast two or possibly three unquiet spirits who can be both seen and heard with heavy footsteps, loud noises and sudden whisperings around the inn.

The previous managers began to experience some unusual events soon after they moved in. One night the landlady was on the upstairs landing when she heard someone call her into an empty bedroom. Knowing that all the rooms were empty, she hesitantly entered the room to find no one there.

Sure that she had made a mistake she thought no more about it until a few nights later when, sitting in front of the downstairs fire waiting for her husband to return after walking the dogs, she felt an alien presence in the room. She turned round and saw to her dismay a dim figure standing at her shoulder. A few seconds later the spirit disappeared.

A further unexplained event was connected to an old blackboard discovered in the barn which, at some time in the past, had shown the prices of various drinks. As expected, letters and numbers were missing and some time was spent

cleaning it and replacing the missing pieces for use in the bar.

After locking the board securely in the barn for the night the landlord came down next morning to find that the same pieces were missing as before and were nowhere to be found. The barn was locked just as he had left it the previous evening.

The main haunting at this time seemed to take place in the corridor and toilets by the old entrance to the inn, now unused. Although always locked at the end of the day, the sound of bitter fighting and violent noise has been heard there late at night, unsettling the dog to such an extent that he had to be dragged into the ladies' part of the cloakrooms when accompanying the landlord on his late night rounds.

This happened one night when the landlady's daughter was sitting chatting to her mother after closing, their Doberman lying quietly beside them. Suddenly the dog's hackles rose and as it dashed to the door the noise began again. Hastily, and certainly courageously, the two ladies opened the door but as they did so the sounds suddenly ceased.

A reputedly haunted inn would not be the same without some form of poltergeist activity and the *Monk & Minstrel* is no exception. At times customers have reported being pushed on the back although no one was near at the time, while bar staff would hear themselves called from the back bar only to find that when they arrived the bar was empty. On one occasion all the brasses in the inn fell from the walls at the same time and, while the inn fronts a busy road, there was no traffic passing at the time.

The present landlord has heard knocking during the night on the bedroom door, and there have been occasions when his gun dog barks frantically at something or someone unseen, usually at about 3 a.m. The cloakroom still appears to be affected by unusual events, for a customer making up her face found the taps to have a mind of their own as they suddenly turned themselves on.

There's one story, leaving much room for speculation, of what took place one night after closing time. Apparently an old cellar lies under the front part of the inn and at 2 a.m. two members of staff, having decided to open it up, began breaking up the concrete floor. The reasons for this nocturnal activity have never been fully explained but it is said that they saw something which set them screaming and brought the landlord rushing downstairs. As he was to say later, "I have never seen anyone so frightened."

The unpleasant sequel to this tale is that they both refused to work at the inn any longer and some months later the woman, who never spoke again, committed suicide.

Since then supernatural events have apparently become less frequent, although the present landlord is sometimes aware of footsteps walking along the upstairs landing and then coming to a halt where the beginnings of an old staircase used to be. The flight of stairs has been blocked off for many years; perhaps the footsteps belong to an inhabitant who knew the house well … a long time ago.

DUKE'S ARMS
Kettering

Over the centuries, wise innkeepers have shown loyalty to the local aristocracy by displaying that family's coat of arms. The name on this inn probably referred to the Duke of Buccleuch whose home is Boughton House and whose estate paid for the rent and upkeep of a row of almshouses built in 1688. These almshouses accommodated six widows or aged people nominated by the Duke.

From 1667 until 1879 the *Duke's Arms* stood at the top of Market Street, but the event which triggered off the following supernatural events took place in 1700 when a group of soldiers were staying at the inn. It is recorded that the youngest of them, a drummer boy, got into an argument and, after being dragged into an alley beside the inn, was foully done to death, whether by his comrades in arms or by others is not documented. It is said that the ghost of the drummer boy has haunted the building and its environs ever since.

However, it was not until the early part of the 20th century that we hear any more of the young soldier. By the 1930s a

The old *Duke's Arms* which once stood in the Market Square.

newsagents stood on the site of the inn, part of which incorporated the old alleyway where the murder had taken place,
and peculiar events began to occur. An eerie atmosphere was
often sensed in the shop, especially in the room which had been
the alleyway, while the owner experienced unusual drops in
temperature and strange noises for which there was no
explanation. It was a ghost that nobody saw.

The odd incidents continued and in 1959, when a Mr Wells
took over the business, the disturbances reached a peak. The
staff began to experience frightening knockings and unusual
noises from a store room upstairs, possibly the same room
where earlier a dagger had been found hidden in the brickwork.

The continuing noises frightened the young assistants to
such an extent that they would only go into the store room in
pairs. One courageous young lady, who was persuaded to
remain behind to take stock, worked until midnight at which
point the door suddenly flew open on its own and she fled from
the shop.

In 1987 the premises became part of a shopping develop-
ment and the disturbances ceased. Perhaps the drummer boy,
unable to compete with the tumult of a modern shopping mall,
has decided that after 300 years it is time for a rest.

FOX & HOUNDS
Kingsthorpe

This inn lies on the Harborough Road out of Northampton with a sign of a happy fox running in an opposite direction to the pack of hounds. Different!

The inn is only slightly connected to the supernatural occurrence which takes us back to the bitter winter of 1940, when Britain was on the brink of losing the war, and hard frost and deep snow blanketed the country.

One evening a Mr George Dobbs made up his mind to visit his local pub. As he ploughed his way through the drifts of snow on the slope which led up to the cemetery he noticed a car driving slowly towards him at about 15 miles an hour, its wheels settling into the deep frozen ruts which covered the road. At this time of night, in these conditions and with petrol being so scarce, this was an unusual sight.

The cemetery gates near to where George
Dobbs saw the phantom cyclist.

Looking more closely he suddenly saw, outlined against the
car's dim headlights, the moving figure of a cyclist struggling to
keep his balance on the treacherous surface of the road. As
George continued on his way he realised that for one foolish
moment he had actually thought the cyclist had no head. Of
course, it was probably the way the man had wrapped himself
up against the cold or even a trick of the headlights as they
came up behind the bike.

Suddenly he realised that the car, getting ever nearer to the
cyclist, showed no sign of slowing down, while the rider,
fighting desperately to keep his balance, seemed oblivious of
the vehicle behind him. Then the car was past George, carrying
on its way towards Market Harborough and with horror he

ran, slipping and sliding towards where the collision must have taken place, fully expecting to see a broken, twisted shape on the snow. Reaching the place where he had last seen the cyclist he crossed and recrossed the road, even searching further into the verges in case the body had been flung to the side. But there was nothing, no smashed cycle and no broken body, just the sound of the wind and the snow shifting slowly in the grasses and hedges which lined the road.

Upset and frightened George made his way as quickly as he could to the warmth and comfort of the *Fox & Hounds*, but was haunted by the thought that he had missed the cyclist who might be lying injured beside the road. Hurrying back to the spot he combed the area back and forth again until he was finally convinced that there was no one there, and returned home, a bewildered man but with the faith in his own eyesight unshaken.

And there the story would have ended except that almost two years later George was at the bar in the *Fox & Hounds* and the talk turned to the supernatural. Diffidently he mentioned his experience of 1940 which made little impression on the company until one of the oldest customers, a Mr 'Lid' Green, for many years the local grave digger, leaned forward in his chair and said, "That was old ...... I buried him about 25 years ago. There was deep snow at the time and he was knocked off his bike just by the cemetery gates. I remember it well for in the crash his head was torn off."

THE OLD RED LION
Litchborough

The heraldic sign on this inn, sometimes called the 'ancient red lion', has been in use since about the 15th century for it belonged to the popular John of Gaunt, fourth son of King Edward III. Then, in the early 19th century, when more of the population were becoming literate, it became the fashion to add names to the signs and for one reason or another sign painters often preferred the word 'old' to 'ancient'.

Although not strictly a story of a haunted inn this tale should be a warning to anyone tempted to take a revenge on the dead, for in the 19th century *The Old Red Lion*, standing opposite the parish church of St Martin's in Litchborough, saw the beginning of certain events which were to lead to a tragedy.

One night a group of locals were enjoying a drink in the inn, and gradually their conversation centred on 'Old Albert' a villager who had died and been buried in the churchyard earlier that day. While most spoke only good of the old man, a certain George Bates leapt to his feet and accused his comrades of hypocrisy for everyone knew that Albert had been a miserable waster and, "They were all better off without him."

One of the company, tired of George's ranting, suggested that, as he hated the dead man so much, why not take the sword hanging above the fireplace, go over to the churchyard and thrust it into the old man's grave "as tho' through his heart." George, his courage fuelled by alcohol, snatched the sword and disappeared into the dark, not to return that night.

No one thought any more of his disappearance that night, for the inn was warm and cosy and the ale was going down well. Little did they imagine that George would never be seen alive again.

Next morning the local gravedigger arriving at the churchyard discovered George's body, his face contorted in

The Old Red Lion on the Litchborough Road.

fear, lying across Albert's grave, his hands frozen to the old sword which had been thrust through his tailcoat and into the grave.

The doctor's verdict on the death was a heart attack brought on by terror and, after hearing what had taken place in the inn the previous night, it was generally assumed that George, thrusting the sword into the soil, had also pinned his tailcoat to the ground. Unable to get away he had believed, in his drunken state, that the corpse was holding him back and died of fright.

It was a sober group of villagers who gathered in *The Old Red Lion* the following night.

There are others, of course, who think differently and murmur about the dangers of speaking ill of the dead, especially so loudly and in such close proximity to the deceased.

St Martin's in Litchborough,
across the road from the inn.

THE SNOOTY FOX
Lowick

From 1702 onwards this establishment was known as The White Horse. *Although the badge was the standard of the Saxons and a device of the House of Hanover it is possible that it took its name from a legend dating back nearly 400 years. Now it has succumbed to the vogue of breweries to adopt new trendy names, hence the snappy inn sign.*

The story of the white horse goes back to a time just after Naseby when the remnants of the Royalist army were running for their lives and it tells of a knight, fleeing to his home near Lowick on a badly wounded horse. The animal, with a pistol ball in its chest, struggled gamely on, but as they got near to Lowick he stumbled, throwing his master into the mill pond where he drowned. At one time this was known as 'Knight's Pond'. The horse continued on his way home only to fall and die a few yards away from shelter.

Over the years many people claim to have heard slow hoofbeats late at night passing their cottage door, but very few have admitted to drawing the curtains to see the white horse pass by.

The village of Lowick, once standing deep in the heart of Rockingham Forest, has been a part of the Drayton estate for many centuries. Today, with its medieval church of St Peters and the old cottages with their Collyweston slated roofs, it is the epitome of a Northamptonshire village.

The building dates back to the 15th century and was at one time the home of the Duchess of Peterborough and the manor house of the village. Then by 1702 documents mention it as being an inn. With its flagstone floor, carved beams and attractive stone staircase leading up to a turret it

This circular staircase is an attractive feature of the inn.

could be mistaken for the old manor ... apart from the sign.

There have been only three odd incidents in the Snooty Fox, which for a building of this age is unusual. I have been told that in 1997, when the inn was closed, a recent owner saw a figure in a long white gown walking in the inn, while three years later a man talking to a woman at the bar turned to order a drink and on turning back found that she had disappeared.

The most recent report is one which took place in 2003 when a chef woke to find himself pinned to the bed. By who or what there is no record but presumably it was something unpleasant or the story would have been forgotten long ago.

Nothing appears to have been witnessed of late, and that is all I know of any supernatural activity at *The Snooty Fox*. It is, however, a pleasant, friendly pub; you will enjoy your meal.

THE AUCTIONEERS
Northampton

At one time it was common practice for all businesses to display descriptive trade signs, but now save for a few exceptions it is just the brewing trade which keeps the tradition alive, and often their signs are today without historical association.

At one time fairs held in the town of Northampton took place in the church and churchyard of All Saints, but by 1235 they had become so rowdy that Henry III ordered them to be held instead "in a waste and empty place to the north of the church." These fairs were the origins of the present-day market and the site became what the historian Morton described in 1712 as "The Market Hill [Square] … lookt upon as the finest in Europe, a fair, spacious, open ground."

Since *The Auctioneers* opened on the west side of the Market Square in December 1994, what can only be described as bizarre occurrences have taken place with apparently more that one spirit haunting the 18th-century building; for medieval singing has been heard in an empty storeroom downstairs as well as the sound of footfalls coming from deserted rooms.

As with many old inns the cellar is reported to be the main area of haunting, for staff often found that bottles were being moved from their original crated positions and discovered lying around haphazardly. At one time this event took place in an eerie silence while a member of staff was working at the other end of the cellar.

On another occasion the deputy manager, staying alone in the building, was just about to go to bed one night when he noticed the airing cupboard door swing quietly open and then close of its own accord. Deciding that 'discretion' in this instance was 'the better part of valour', he went straight to bed where, presumably, he pulled the bedclothes over his head and went to sleep … and who could blame him?

In the same room another occupant had a far more terrifying experience for, turning over in bed, she saw what seemed to be the top half of a man floating above her. Unable to take her eyes off him, she watched as he began turning to look at her, but then, to her great relief, he ... "just disappeared".

The next to be heard of anything supernatural was in 1999 when the new manager and his wife began experiencing the sound of screams in the night and the recurring sobbing of a woman. Added to this was the noise of beer barrels being rolled round the cellar floor while a woman, dressed in old-fashioned clothes, would appear on the stairs and then fade away to nothing.

However, far more uncanny, was the smell of smoke which would often permeate the building, for the pub is situated at the place which took the brunt of the Great Fire of Northampton in 1675 when it is recorded that barrels of beer were rolled out of the cellar to save them.

The inn is also very near to the site of another, once known as *The Shoulder of Mutton*, which burned down on 16th February 1792 with tragic results. The landlady, her five children – the oldest only twelve – and two lodgers died in the inferno. As with many buildings of that period, the structure was pred-ominantly wooden and the fire caught hold within minutes, taking neighbours until the next morning to put out the flames. The landlord alone survived – unable to save his family, he climbed out of the attic and over adjoining roofs to safety.

It has been said that on occasions over the last two hundred years, some have seen the spectre of the innkeeper, a broken-hearted man, roaming the area while the cries of the children can be heard coming from what was once their home.

Since then the hauntings appear to have died away. Perhaps the spirits prefer old madrigals to the recorded music now played in the inn and feel even their best endeavours would pale beside the viewing to be had on the screen attached to the walls.

SHIPMAN'S
Northampton

Once known as The White Hart, *the inn, which was founded in the latter half of the 18th century, stands beside the Market Square with one entrance in the Drapery and another in a little jetty called Drum Lane. This shortcut leading to the Square has been in use for hundreds of years, changing very little along the way. About 120 years ago the inn was taken over and managed by two brothers, John and Walter Shipman, hence the present name.*

Shipman's is an archetypical town inn whose exterior has changed little over the centuries. In these days of 'trendy makeovers' the interior with its old beams, flagged floor and layout of cosy alcoves gives its customers a welcome as they walk through the door.

Shipman's inn has at least one troublesome spook whose activities have puzzled staff and customers alike for years.

When the present landlady took over and heard stories about a ghost who stalked the inn, she was fairly sceptical until a photograph of the interior showed a ghostly figure standing next to the fruit machine. Since then mysterious footsteps have been heard on the stairs with strange noises coming from the bathroom, while the family's dog refused to enter the Barrel Bar and has been found with its hair on end growling at 'nothing'.

Customers have complained about full pint glasses sliding off tables, and at one stage sticky pads were used to solve the problem. This, unfortunately, proved no deterrent to the spirit who started doing the same thing at another table.

However, it was not only poltergeist activity which affected the inn, for members of the family have seen the figure of a man with a walking stick in their bedrooms, while a barman reported the sound of a walking stick knocking on his door.

It is thought that all these activities can be traced back to a man called Harry Franklin who managed the inn at the turn of the 19th century. He is said to have committed suicide by slitting his own throat in such a manner that it took him a week to die.

I am informed that Harry has not made himself known recently but perhaps he feels that after such a good innings it is time to retire to wherever old landlords go.

The staircase behind the bar at *Shipman's*

THE WHITEHILLS
Northampton

This spacious modern building, named after the area where it was built, just off the Harborough Road, became an inn in 1935.

Although this Northampton pub is comparatively modern it seems to harbour one or two spirits, not necessarily of the friendly kind.

At one time staff would joke about the spook which gave clocks and electrical equipment a mind of their own, but when two barmen claimed they had seen a figure surrounded by a green haze, things began to get serious. One visitation took place in the cellar when a part-time student who had gone down there returned so terrified that other staff said, "He looked as white as a sheet." Whether or not the young man actually saw anything supernatural or had been spooked by recent reports we shall never know.

The present landlord has been in residence for seventeen years and admits that at first he was sceptical of the stories he heard about spooky goings on – until, that is, he met an exorcist.

This pleasant gentleman, with a glass full to the brim, stood chatting to the landlord until mine host broke off the conversation and turned away to pull a pint for another customer. A few seconds later on turning back he discovered that not only had the 'exorcist' disappeared but his glass was completely empty. There was no sign of the customer anywhere in or out of the inn.

The present ghost's domain appears to be in the cellar where a large keg known to be at least half full became empty in a matter of seconds, while the landlord's dog, with the sensitivity of its kind, refuses to set foot down there.

As far as I know there is nothing in the inn's history to account for any of the odd happenings there, but a haunting has to have a beginning ... doesn't it?

THE WIG & PEN
Northampton

The Wig and Pen in St Giles Street, Northampton, started life in the early 18th century as a coffee house called The Plasterers Arms. *Around 1720 it changed to an inn becoming* The Black Lion, *taking its name and sign from the great Welsh leader Owen Glendower, the self-styled Prince of Wales, who defeated England's Henry IV three times in battle.*

The Wig & Pen is a narrow building standing on St Giles Street not far from the lovely old Royal Theatre. In the 18th century, strolling players used to lodge there, amongst them members of the family of Roger Kemble, head of a famous theatrical family and father to the actress Sarah Siddons. It is also said to be the most haunted inn in the county.

The many eerie happenings connected to this inn are well documented over the years by landlords, customers and workmen. The main haunting is said to derive from an appalling double murder which took place in 1892, when Andrew McRae, a married man, was sentenced to death for killing his mistress, Annie Pritchard, and their baby. After the murders, he boiled up Annie's head and arms along with the baby in a boiler, which was also used to boil the bacon he sold on Northampton Market. At that time the warehouse stood in Dychurch Lane, which still runs along the back of the inn.

There was no question of him getting away with the crime for, soon after the murders, a headless and armless body wrapped in a sack was found in a ditch on the way to East Haddon. The sack was stencilled 'E. M. McRae, Northampton' and led the police first to a bacon-curing establishment and then to a stall in the Market Square where McRae was arrested. On the Christmas Eve of the same year he was found guilty of murder and sentenced to death.

However, that was not to be the end of the story for, soon after, travellers on the road to East Haddon claimed to have been followed by footsteps 'to their great discomfort'.

Gradually around the county the belief grew that these footfalls belonged to the murdered woman, following in the footsteps of her killer on his way back to Northampton.

The grave of Annie Pritchard, as it was, at East Haddon.
(Courtesy: *Chronicle & Echo*)

Annie was buried at East Haddon near where her body was found, and it is rumoured that not only does her face appear on the gravestone but if you walk there you will hear footsteps, but find nobody around.

Most of the hauntings in the inn seem to be centred on the great, square cellars which extend under St Giles Street. With ancient stone walls and vaulted roofs they are believed to be part of the old underground passageways of Northampton, possessing secrets known only to themselves.

A previous licensee, along with his barman, watched in disbelief as 'fog and mist' emerged from the cellar walls only to disappear seconds later, while another landlord encountered such a strong sensation of 'freezing' that he was unable to continue working down there.

Dogs, sensitive to the presence of the paranormal, are particularly affected by the cellars, refusing to enter even the newer, higher ones. In February 1973 the new licensee entered the cellars with his Alsatian puppy for the first time. "It sniffed around then suddenly stopped dead at one end of the cellar looking towards a wall," from which, barking hysterically, it backed away. The puppy would never go down into the cellar again and was said to have died soon after.

Poltergeist activity has also taken place there with heavy barrels being moved around, and on one occasion a previous landlord discovered that sometime between a Sunday afternoon and 7 p.m. the same evening a 220lb barrel had been removed from a ramp and placed in the gangway almost blocking the entrance. No one else was in the building and the barrel had been moved without a sound being heard.

The spirits' domain is not confined to the lower levels of *The Wig & Pen*, for upstairs doors have been flung open as if someone was passing through in a hurry, while draughts, their origins unknown, rustle the hair and papers of the customers.

Mysterious mists appear and shadowy figures move behind a glass screen at one end of a bar. Other shapes walk along a passageway to disappear through a wall where once there was a doorway now bricked up, and on one occasion a member of staff heard, late at night, the eerie sound of a young voice singing 'Oranges and Lemons'.

Footsteps have been heard coming from upstairs, perhaps made by the heavily-built man with a large black dog who appeared in a bedroom, or the woman dressed in a riding habit, who has been seen on the stairs.

On another occasion a previous licensee and his wife woke at 3 a.m. to see a lady sitting on the end of the bed. We are told that it was a very thin lady with white hair pulled back into a bun while her clothing was dark and in the style of an older age, possibly Victorian. After that first visit the lady could be seen quite regularly around that time in the morning sitting quietly on the bed, disappearing only when an effort was made to engage her in conversation. A harmless, friendly spirit.

In 1993 workmen refitting the inn were puzzled as to why lights were switching off and on, and tools disappeared, only to appear much later in the same spot. At one time a plasterer working upstairs heard footsteps below him. Going downstairs to investigate, he found the building empty.

Some years ago the *Chronicle and Echo* interviewed five past landlords who claimed to have had uncanny experiences during their tenure, while more recently a local psychic research group, investigating the paranormal events, recorded seeing a peculiar light in the cellar as well as hearing the sound of a baby crying.

The many and varied sounds and sightings which have taken place at this inn over such a long period of time make logical explanations difficult, but then, whoever ruled that hauntings had to be logical?

Finally, a member of staff recently admitted to me that although she has never seen anything, she feels watched, and makes sure that she is never alone in the pub.

The saga continues.

THE SHIP INN
West Street, Oundle

Sometimes the ship sign is seen on inns which have no obvious connection to the sea. However, the age of this building would seem to link the name with the story of Noah's Ark; a popular sign in the Middle Ages because of its religious connection.

The 14th-century *Ship Inn* was a coaching inn and retains the broad entrance archway through which the stage carrying its weary passengers would arrive. With its bow windows, winding stairs, low beams and panelled rooms, the inn boasts a chequered history as well as a few restless spirits.

The centre of the disturbances appears to be a bedroom where few guests enjoy a good night's rest. According to the present landlord, a sane and level-headed writer who was given this particular bedroom had passed an unpleasant night, and next morning described the room as possessing a restless, disturbing quality.

Apparently, twenty years ago, parapsychologists failed to rid the inn of two apparitions who haunted the bedrooms. One of these spectres may have something to do with a woman found strangled in one of those rooms in the early 19th century. The room where she died was said to remain cold however much the heating was turned up.

Reported sightings have included soldiers and ladies in medieval dress, while staff and visitors alike have been aware of something unseen brushing past them on the stairs. Then there are reports of cold spots appearing in the upper part of the house and in a tiny snug facing onto the street, for which there is no logical reason.

There is the story of a previous landlord who threw himself to his death from an upstairs window, only to be seen rushing through the inn by his horrified successor; and then there is the tale of a landlady at the inn who, after setting the table for tea one evening, walked out never to return. Of course this latter tale adds nothing to the reputed hauntings, perhaps the lady just wanted a change of lifestyle, quickly.

THE TALBOT
Oundle

Formerly known as The Tabret, *a form of tabard which was a sleeveless coat worn by heralds, the inn was founded in 638 AD by a group of monks as a hostel for pilgrims and wayfarers. Eventually the name was changed to* The Talbot, *a popular breed of hunting dog marked with black spots over the body and legs. The sign was also the crest of the Talbot family, the Earls of Shrewsbury, and many of today's signs are believed to come from that source rather than from the now extinct breed of dog.*

Surrounded on three sides by the River Nene, Oundle is one of the historic towns of Northamptonshire. A walk down the main street will take you past timeless 17th- and 18th-century buildings, old streets and little alleyways until you come to the Market Square and the ancient *Talbot Hotel* with its grey stone front, oak beams and panelled rooms where wanders the spirit of Mary Queen of Scots.

Mary Queen of Scots.
(Courtesy: *The Talbot Hotel*)

Fotheringhay Castle, lying approximately four miles north of Oundle, was the site of Mary's execution in 1587 and the place where one would expect to encounter her. However, that was demolished years ago leaving just a mound in the grounds of a farmhouse, while many of the castle's stones and furnishings ended up in other locations such as *The Talbot*.

By 1626 the inn was in urgent need of repairs and alterations, and over the next few years it was refurbished in grand style by the landlord, William Whitwell, using stones from the demolished castle to give the inn a new façade. The great horn windows and the panelling in the residents' lounge are also said to have been brought from the castle along with the magnificent oak staircase which once led to the top room of Fotheringhay Castle where Mary was kept under house arrest. The small gate, halfway up the stairs, was the boundary of her prison confines, beyond which she was never allowed to walk.

We are told that at Fotheringhay three hundred guests gathered in the great hall to witness Mary's execution. They waited in silence as the royal lady dressed in black with a red petticoat, which was the symbol of a Catholic martyr, began to descend the stairs in a manner befitting a Queen, and they watched as she panicked and had to be dragged the rest of the way to the block which was set up in the hall. It is said that the mark of a crown, still visible in the wood, is an imprint left from her ring as she clutched at the balustrade.

One further connection to Mary is the well-documented fact that the executioner who was to behead her lodged at *The Talbot* the night before the execution. He "partook of pigeon pie, drank a quart of best ale and made a merry discourse with the serving girl til the early hours of the morning."

The next morning, not surprisingly, he botched his job, severing the Queen's head from her body only on the third attempt.

The stair gate through which Mary was not allowed to pass.

On the staircase of the inn, a scene of much fear and unhappiness, some visitors have been aware of the strong smell of perfume and others have been unable to take pictures because of their cameras jamming, or the film has come out blank. Others have felt a sense of chilling unease as they descend, passing the horn windows which let light onto the oak staircase and from where the figure of a woman has been seen staring down into the yard.

Further supernatural activity focuses on two of the bedrooms on the top floor, in which occupants have been awakened by a woman crying and have witnessed a swirling white mist. Guests in a particular room have often independently complained of feeling cold in the night. Some guests have seen a figure in a long black dress standing at the foot of the bed, while one was woken by a weight, like the pressure of hands, pushing her down into the sheets. Too terrified to move she lay there until, eventually, the pressure eased.

Perhaps it is not surprising that this room is only used when the hotel is completely full.

Further examples of reported supernatural activity are the sounds of sobbing and wailing in the empty room and the echo of passing footsteps with no one around to make them, while heavy furniture is moved about by an invisible hand, and a picture depicting Mary's execution has been known to jump off the wall.

It appears that stones and furnishings were not the only things that Whitwell, the landlord, transferred from Fotheringhay Castle.

Another type of haunting is associated with Dodd's Yard, which still stands at the rear of the inn. Given to the inn in 1547 as a right of access, it first became famous in the middle of the 17th century when drumming in the manner of a march was heard coming from a well that stood in the middle of the yard.

About that time a visitor recorded, "It is said to be very ominous, and always precedes some great accident ... and that it beat for a fortnight the latter end of the last month and the beginning of this and was heard in the very same manner before the late King's death by Cromwell, the King's coming in and the fire of London."

Dodd's Yard, renamed Drummingwell Lane.

One assumes that no other event thereafter was thought by the drummer to be worthy of his skill, for towards the end of that century the phenomenon ceased altogether, and eventually the opportunity was taken, possibly with great relief, to fill in the well and lay the drummer, if that was what he was, to rest.

Dodd's Yard or Drummingwell Lane, as it has been re-named, is now a peaceful courtyard which provides access to the rear of *The Talbot*.

The Talbot in May 1931.

THE SPREAD EAGLE
Piddington

This sign depicts the king of the birds and is found frequently on banners and shields, and it goes as far back as the Roman period when it was borne facing front with its wings extended – the Spread Eagle. With a Romano British site having been found near to the village, the sign is certainly appropriate.

The inn dates back to 1765 and is said to be haunted by a friendly ghost called Daniel. George Daniel Howes was the landlord of the inn for 43 years from *c.*1890 and some say he prefers to 'hang around', keeping an eye on the business.

THE THORNHILL ARMS
Rushton

Overlooking the cricket pitch and the lovely old church of All Saints,
The Thornhill Arms *takes its present name from the family who*
owned Rushton Hall from the mid-1800s until well into the 20th
century.

For hundreds of years the history of Rushton has been tied up
with the Tresham family. Thomas, who built the Hall, was the
grandson of the last Lord Prior in England of the Knights
Hospitallers and it was his nephew Francis who would become
heavily involved in the Gunpowder Plot to the ruin of the
family. As a result of his treasonable activities the estates
became forfeit to the crown and the family descended into
poverty, with the last of the line dying childless and in debt two
generations later.

Surprisingly it is not the Treshams who haunt *The Thornhill
Arms* but two or more spirits of a different sort. One first
appeared to the landlady, Sue Haynes, soon after she and her
husband Gary took over the inn, a bizarre occurrence which
turned out to be the first of many.

One Sunday, late at night, Mrs Haynes suddenly became
aware of a woman dressed in an old-fashioned cloak 'sort of
floating past' the area between the doorway and the toilet. As
she said, "I couldn't believe it. I had heard about the place
being haunted but I never believed in ghosts until I saw one
myself."

There is no clue as to the lady's identity in the pub's history
but it seems likely that she roamed the upper floors as well, for
soon after the family moved in their pet dog began to act
strangely, refusing to cross part of the first floor landing
however much he was coaxed.

Apparently this went on for five or six weeks until one day
he was found barking frantically and staring at the same place
in the corner of the landing. Presumably his challenge had a

successful outcome for after that he always moved across the landing quite freely.

Further odd occurrences include several unexplained cold spots near the main entrance to the inn, while heavy doors in the cellar slam continuously or are found locked through no normal agency. One of these doors sporting a big, heavy old-fashioned lock refused to open even when a crowbar was used on it. Eventually the staff gave up and were turning away when, to their amazement, the heavy key twisted in the lock and flew across the room while the door swung silently open.

Like many old hauntings the reasons behind them have been long forgotten but *The Thornhill Arms* has a strong connection to the English Civil War. It is said that the bodies of soldiers were brought here and laid in the cold cellar before being taken along to the church of All Saints for burial. In fact, I am told that body-length slates still remain in the cellar.

It is recorded that the bodies were taken for burial after dark so that the local inhabitants wouldn't be upset. Unfortunately the noise of the carts trundling down the village street at night with their grisly loads disturbed the villagers' sleep and they complained loudly to those in charge of the burial detail. It is said that a tunnel was hastily dug from the inn to the church and the bodies moved to their final resting places in that way, disturbing no one.

Part of the remains of Pipewell Abbey.

The whereabouts of this tunnel is now lost in the mists of time, if indeed it existed at all.

Although not strictly connected to *The Thornhill Arms*, a very persistent and eerie phantom haunts the area. Known as the Barford Monk and well documented as far back as the time of horse-drawn transport, the hooded spectre will appear suddenly on the road in front of a vehicle which invariably appears to run it down. When the horrified driver runs to give assistance, the road is always empty, there is no one there.

Quite recently a lone woman driver encountered the monk on the road, and white and shaking rushed into *The Thornhill Arms* saying that she had seen someone step in front of her car and, sure that she had knocked him over, got out only to find an empty road with no sign of a body.

The monk is said to be connected to the lost hamlet of Barford which was demolished in the 16th century to make way for sheep pasture. Standing on the opposite side of the road from Newton, its small chapel was served by a monk from the Cistercian Abbey at Pipewell, north of Rushton. Pipewell, a village community of nine in the Domesday Book, was eliminated by the predatory Cistercians, who placed their abbey at the east end of the village in 1143, presumably on the premise of 'the greatest good for the greatest number'.

As late as 1845 a footpath went from the remains of Pipewell to Barford Bridge, known locally as the Monk's Walk. Along this single track road, usually at dawn or dusk the phantom appears, gliding over the fields between Barford Bridge and the lonely church of Newton in the Willows.

However, there is more to the hauntings then a wandering monk, for on the stretch of dual carriageway between Kettering and Corby, the A6003, a white silvery figure has been seen to glide across the road and solitary drivers have suddenly looked in their rear view mirrors to find they are carrying a spectral passenger.

Then, in 1984, a woman driving on her own saw in her rear mirror, as though through a mist, what she took to be a man's face. Wisely she didn't stop to investigate and arriving home in a panic was relieved to find the 'passenger' gone, her car empty. About the same time a police sergeant experienced the same phenomena but immediately stopped the car and, on checking the back seat, found nothing and no one there.

Many people are convinced that that length of carriageway hides some terrifying secrets, for the road has been the scene of too many accidents as cars have stopped, skidded or turned over for no reason.

However, sightings of the phantom monk seem to get fewer and fewer as time goes by. Perhaps he has been frightened away by all the building work which is taking place on that stretch of road ... or perhaps not.

So let us leave the last word to an elderly lady who has lived near the bridge over the A6003 for many years. She believes that "If it's your turn to meet the ghost, there's nothing you can do about it."

THE SAMUEL PEPYS
Slipton

Originally known as The Red Cow, *this inn is now named after the famous diarist of the 17th century.*

The Samuel Pepys is a 400-year-old coaching inn which stands north off the A14 between Twywell and Sudborough. Situated in the village on the junction of Main Street and Slipton Lane it retains the atmosphere of an old English pub.

Nothing is known for certain about the spectres who haunt this popular inn, but a good beginning is the fact that many years ago a landlord murdered his wife here, before sealing her in the pub chimney. She was presumably disinterred at some time and her murderer punished, but perhaps her spirit still feels the need to haunt the place where she died so violently.

Certainly an unidentified figure has been seen by at least one previous landlord who, sitting alone at night going over some accounts, became aware of a figure by the fireplace. Knowing that he had locked up for the night and was alone in the building, he hastily switched on the bar lights, but the bar was empty with nothing to account for the clearly seen figure that had stood hunched by the fireplace.

It is also said the ghost of a lady dressed in blue wanders the inn. Whether this is the shade of the murdered woman is not known and sightings have become fewer with each passing year.

THE VANE ARMS
Sudborough

The inn took its name from a local landowning family of Sudborough and Brigstock.

This was a favourite pub for the crews of the American Air Force in World War II. On the eve of a mission the crews of the B17s would place a coin in one of the numerous cracks of the beam over the inglenook fireplace as a token of good luck. If the crew did not return from their raid, their friends would flatten the coin over the beam.

As there was no transport to the inn, the men of the 8th Air Force would take a short cut across the fields, via Old Head Wood and Grafton Park Wood. Since then it is said that the figure of a man dressed in the uniform of an airman has been seen walking through the fields towards Sudborough from the direction of the Grafton Underwood to Brigstock road. Whether this is indeed a member of one of the bomber crews retracing the journeys he made so many years ago is left to supposition.

PLUME OF FEATHERS
Weedon

Originally the badge of the King of Bohemia, this sign was taken by the Black Prince after defeating Bohemia in battle. Although the three ostrich plumes and the 'Ich Dien' is still the crest of the Prince of Wales, naming it the Prince of Wales Feathers is a misnomer for it is the badge of the heir apparent, whether or not he holds the title Prince of Wales.

Although this inn dates back to the early 17th century, the earliest recorded reference to it is in 1759 when a John Smith is recorded as its publican.

With a reputation for being haunted which goes back to 1650, The *Plume of Feathers* is said to possess at least five unquiet spirits. For the landlord at that time, Paul Breese, it all began in October 1997 after the inn had been refurbished and a new restaurant built. Fruit machine wheels began to spin of their own accord, while doors in the inn started to open and slam shut, and plates and chairs flew across the rooms. Eerie groans and giggles began to echo from empty rooms, and lights were switched on and off with the result that the landlord had to keep replacing light bulbs at the rate of between ten and twenty a week.

One of the phantoms is said to be an old man, a former landlord named George, who would sit in certain parts of the pub at certain times. His identity came to light when his 88-year-old niece recognised him from the description given of his clothes, "… with the spats and garters. He was a bit of a dandy." George ran the pub along with his mother and brother at the turn of the century, dying in 1920, and as his niece commented, "He must have been there quite a long time. I don't know why."

The pub cleaner at this time was never worried by his presence until one day she reported that "he (George) was playing the fruit machine and there was this shadow over it. It was terrifying … I left."

Another spirit is said to be that of a highwayman, possibly one of the notorious

George, who helped manage the inn at the turn of the last century. (Courtesy: *Plume of Feathers*)

Culworth Gang who haunted the south of Northamptonshire in the 17th and 18th centuries. It is also worth mentioning that in the early 18th century two notorious highwaymen – Dick Turpin and Jack Sheppard – were spreading terror from Whittlebury Forest northwards; their favourite targets being stagecoaches on the Oxford to Peterborough run.

Certainly there have been at least two unexplained sightings of a man on horseback on the Daventry to Weedon Road, known as the old highwayman's route. Sighted by a motorist on the Weedon to Daventry road one night some years ago, a mounted man in an old-fashioned brown coat and a big raised hat appeared on the road in front of him. The horse, covered in mud, was tossing its head and chomping at the bit as though it had suddenly been pulled up. As the driver stopped the car,

The *Plume of Feathers* in 1916.

the horse and rider turned and walked slowly across the road in front of him, fading into air as they reached the hedge.

A similar apparition was witnessed by a family of five who were on their way to Daventry from Northampton in the middle of the afternoon. Overtaking a man on horseback wearing a long cloak, the driver, who intended to acknowledge him, was surprised to see the figure just disappear.

Neither of the motorists was able to make out the features of the man on horseback and as far as I know there have been no sightings of him in recent years. Perhaps he prefers the comforts of the inn to long hours in the saddle.

Members of the well-established Phenomena Investigation Group who have researched the unexplained events taking place in the inn, name the remaining spectres as a young boy, a serving wench and a little girl. With all these extra guests, the *Plume of Feathers* may well be one of the more haunted inns in the county.

Weedon stands on a major road junction between the A5 and the A45 with the Grand Union Canal passing through the village and also boasts two other inns which are reputedly haunted. Legend tells us that *The New Inn* in the High Street and overlooking the Grand Union Canal is supposedly haunted by a spirit named Gertie. Nothing much is known of her except that, according to the customers, she appears to enjoy throwing bottles and glasses around the bar.

THE HIND HOTEL
Wellingborough

The Hind Hotel, *a Grade II listed building, is named after the 'hind passant d'or', the golden deer which formed part of the coat of arms of Sir Christopher Hatton. Known as the 'dancing chancellor' and a great favourite of Elizabeth I, his fortunes were tied to Northamptonshire where he owned the great houses of Kirby and Holdenby.*

For hundreds of years there has been a building on the site of the present hotel, one of which provided hospitality and refuge for visitors, especially those travelling to the nearby ecclesiastical college which belonged to Crowland Abbey in Lincolnshire. Tradition has it that there were tunnels linking the hospice with both the college and the church of All Hallows, although nothing has ever been proven.

Much of the haunting connected to *The Hind Hotel* centres around Oliver Cromwell, leader of the parliamentary army during the English Civil War. While it is more likely that the contingent of troops who passed through the town on their way to Naseby were under the command of General Fairfax, there is a tradition that Cromwell himself supped and stayed at

A nineteenth-century advertisement for *The Hind Hotel*.

the inn, even though the historian Francis Whelan tells us that
the building was under reconstruction at the time.

Supporting the tradition is a signed letter in Cromwell's
handwriting asking that "forage maight be prepared there for
his troops at that juncture". This document is reported to have
been in the possession of Mr Mackworth Dolben of Finedon
and exhibited in Wellingborough in the mid-19th century.

A rather unfriendly poltergeist is said to have been around
for three hundred years and is referred to as the White Lady.
This phantom appears in late September and early October
between the hours of ten and midnight and is reputed to be a
serving 'wench' strangled after overhearing the Parliamentarians planning the strategy for the Battle of Naseby.

There is also a Grey Lady appearing mostly in Room No. 3
which overlooks Sheep Street and Market Street from a fine
bow window. On at least two occasions guests have refused to
spend a night in that room, saying it exuded an eerie and
discomforting atmosphere. In fact one guest, not liking to

change rooms for such a reason, preferred to spend his nights in the reception area, only explaining why as he paid his bill.

Although it is a long time since the Grey Lady made herself known, the present manageress tells me that there are still guests, mainly ladies, who refuse even to go through the door of the room because of the atmosphere. Photographing there, I felt no sense of being watched, although the room had a very quiet, almost

The Cromwell Room, with the entrance to an underground passageway, now blocked off.

oppressive quality. If the lady disliked me invading her privacy, she made no sign. Perhaps she enjoys the publicity.

Another unidentified spirit, though of a more pleasant sort, is that of old Mrs Priddy who roamed the corridors in the first half of the last century. This gentle lady had never been known to harm or disturb anyone and apparently the staff who encountered her would nod and go on their way. It has been some time since Mrs Priddy walked the inn; perhaps she has faded away in a suitably respectable fashion.

More recently a sad story emerged from the history of *The Hind*, for two members of staff had sightings of a ghost of a little girl who centuries ago, it is said, fell down the staircase of the inn to her death. The child has often been seen in the restaurant under one of the tables and also in a corner of the room. Crying has been heard there when the room gets dark, so now a lamp is kept there to comfort her. However, the child is not always sad, for last year a member of staff, alone in the restaurant felt something brush past her and lightly touch her hand, and then came a little giggle.

Some of *The Hind Hotel's* wandering spirits have proved physically dangerous, for in 1978 a reception manageress found herself unable to sleep for the sound of moving furniture next door in the Cromwell Room. The disturbances became more violent and, four months later, when the building was closed for major internal repairs, the new general manager was struck on the head by a flying tumbler and a full bottle of orange, while ashtrays exploded in front of his face.

The three-week closure of the hotel obviously upset one or more of the phantoms because for all that time lights dimmed, flickered and went off, the whole atmosphere being so unpleasant that it lead to the resignation of one of the barmen.

Very few of these phantoms can be identified. All that can be told of them is their behaviour after death, and last Hallowe'en a well-known and respected psychic spent the midnight hours along with others in a room of the hotel. Although no spirit materialized, globes of light were seen, while many felt cold and spoke of an eerie presence in the room.

Although *The Hind Hotel* has been 'smartened up' in keeping with the 21st century, it still retains much of the atmosphere and internal structure of the old inn ... no wonder so many spirits find it difficult to leave.

RAFFERTY'S
Wellingborough

Over the years this 400-year-old inn, standing at the junction of four roads, has been known as The King of Prussia, *then later* The Globe, *showing a sign that was an emblem of Portugal and one which was used to advertise Portuguese wine. Now, suffering from the vogue of breweries to give their premises modern, trendy names, it is called* Rafferty's, *the name deriving from County Donegal and meaning prosperity.*

Up to 1835 this tavern stood at the bottom of Hog Hill, so called because of the Hog Fair which had taken place there for many years. Then the Duke of Gloucester, after staying the night at *The Hind Hotel* en route to Cambridge, was flung from his carriage in front of *The Globe*. The cheering and fanfares stopped as the landlord of the inn rushed to pick up the fallen Prince and send him on his way unscathed. In honour of that incident, Hog Hill was renamed Gloucester Place. This leads into Cambridge Street.

The Globe Inn in 1910.

However, name changes take some getting used to, even those with royal connections, and for some time Gloucester Place remained known by older inhabitants as 'ug 'ill.

This inn has, for many years, reputedly been haunted by a single, unidentified phantom. His appearance is that of a Quaker, or member of the Society of Friends, and is described in exactly the same way by everyone who sees him. Most noticeably he wears a black old-fashioned jacket and white knee-length socks, while moving quietly along the alley at the back of the premises or entering the pub. Some time ago two customers, making their way to the toilet down the narrow stone passage at the rear of the pub, were terrified when they came face to face with the spirit, dressed in the old-fashioned clothing of years ago, and beat a hasty retreat to the comparative safety of the bar.

The spectre will regularly move objects or spirit them away, he slams doors when there is no one near and appears to have a certain sense of humour for he enjoys jamming lavatory doors with some luckless person inside.

The meeting place of The Society of Friends in St John Street.

Why a Quaker? No one knows the reason for his presence. However, it is recorded that that the Society of Friends held meetings in Wellingborough in the early 17th century and that George Fox, the religion's founder, visited Wellingborough in 1655. At that time the Quakers, so called because Fox had told them to "quake at the word of the Lord", were a persecuted minority. All manner of crimes were laid at their door with members often being dragged roughly out of meetings and imprisoned without trial.

However, the passing years brought tolerance, and in 1819 the church of the Society of Friends was built in ancient St John Street. It is there still with its burial ground, laid out in a formal and dignified manner in front of the grey brick chapel, still containing the graves of some of the foremost citizens of that age. The chapel was also a three minutes walk away from *The Globe*.

Although this affable spirit has not been seen for some time, there are customers who say they can occasionally sense a presence in the old alley at the rear of the inn, and hear a quiet chuckle close by.

THE GEORGE INN
Wilby

Although many inns with this name have a sign showing one of the Britain's more popular monarchs, the name on this inn sign shows a picture of George and the Dragon.

The village of Wilby, on the urban edge of Wellingborough, once stood in Rockingham Forest when the woodland stretched as far south as Northampton. Known in the Domesday Book as Wilebi, it came into the hands of Judith, niece of William I and it was she who founded the beautiful little church of St Mary the Virgin which stands in the village.

The George is a lovely old ironstone building dating back to the early 16th century with a barn dating 200 years earlier. Its main entrance fronts onto the old A45 Wellingborough to Northampton Road, while from the more modern extension at the back it overlooks the fields and copses leading to Doddington Ridge.

The inn appears to possess at least one unquiet spirit who has been seen wandering through the bar in daylight when no customers were around. On one occasion a member of staff, seeing the figure of what he believed to be the landlord, called out. To his discomfort, however, the spectre dis-appeared while the landlord's response came from the cellar where he had been working for some time. Perhaps it is the

The front bar
where an unknown figure
has been seen walking.

same spirit who uses the door leading to an upstairs attic which is regularly found open even though the owners keep it locked.

Poltergeist activity includes the violent noise of barrels banging together. This comes from the cellar where the barrels are stored and which are far too heavy to move on their own. The noise was so unpleasant that a previous chef who experi-enced these disturbances refused to enter the cellar again.

Even the great barn doors are not immune from the uncanny events which take place here and I am told that it is possible to hear the click of their heavy latches before they swing open of their own accord two or three times a day, while the barn windows, although left securely fastened, are often found wide open. In spite of careful searches no explanation has been found for these incidents.

Whether any of this has something to do with a previous landlord, known as Mad Jack, is a moot point. Jack Haddon, who kept *The George* during the 1960s, was renowned for his eccentric behaviour. Although he was only in his fifties at that time, he would change into his pyjamas at 10 o'clock every night and continue serving behind the bar. Apparently one of his favourite pastimes was shooting his rifle up the inn chimney in order to clean it. This would invariably result in an avalanche of soot, which covered his customers, along with dead birds and flea-ridden nests.

Although Jack is long gone it appears that he has never been forgotten by some of the older villagers who still arrange to meet their friends at 'Mad Jack's'.

Growing in the grounds of *The George* is an ancient mulberry tree, approximately 450 years old. It is recorded that

on the day before Naseby, Cromwell and his officers left *The Hind* in Wellingborough, and after travelling half a day, held a meeting under a 'mulberry tree'. The timing and the place seem to fit and whatever they discussed certainly did them no disservice on the following day.

The mulberry tree known by some as the 'Hanging Tree'.

However, the tree could have a more gory history for in the village it is also known as the 'Hanging Tree'. Whether it was used for that purpose at one time and is a part of the inn's ghostly past or, more mundanely, it is a name in use generally because of the blood-like juice which runs from the berries, I haven't been able to discover.

The barn where heavy doors swing open of their own accord.

A few facts
about inns past and present

THE OLD FIVE BELLS
[Now known as *The Frog and Fiddler*]
Harborough Road
Kingsthorpe

Years ago when Boughton Green Fair was held, the inn was a popular meeting place for those going to and from the fair. This was because the inn specialised in a sugar drink which was deemed to be invigorating!

THE WHITE HORSE
Kingsthorpe

Apart from being a sporting sign, the white horse was the emblem of the Saxons and, more recently, connected to both innkeepers and farriers.

In the past, English justice was harsh and cruel and this inn's claim to fame was that at one time public burnings took place nearby. Presumably the crowds who came to watch would fortify themselves at the bar before going outside to gape at the spectacle.

THE BANTAM COCK
(Now known as *The Bantam*)
Abington Square
Northampton

It is thought the name derives from the coat of arms of Lady Cockayne which contained three bantam cocks. Lady Cockayne also owned land which adjoined the inn.

Although this building is only 80 years old, a pub of that name has stood on this site since 1486. Standing on open ground it survived the Great Fire of Northampton in 1675 and was able to shelter refugees who had fled for their lives. It also had the distinction of being the last inn out of town and it is said that prisoners were allowed a last drink there before being taken to the Racecourse to be hanged.

THE FLYING HORSE
(Subsequently *The Lord Palmerston Hotel*)
Once on the east side of the Market Square
Northampton

The name of this inn might be connected to the local Racecourse. Most inns stabled horses and it is probable that The Flying Horse *would do so for the racing events.*

In 1760 William Fisher a surgeon and apothecary, grandson of the late Dr Fisher of Olney, advertised that he would be at the inn to dispense medicines prepared by him after the manner of his late grandfather. Of course, these elixirs would cost a certain amount of money but, after all, one had to pay for quality!

The people of the town, knowing him for a 'quack', were not impressed and the adage "like Fisher's pills, out of date" became a Northampton-shire saying.

In 1864, Lord Palmerston, whose wife cut the first sod at the site of the railway station at Towcester, visited Northampton and the inn was renamed *The Lord Palmerston*.

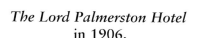

The Lord Palmerston Hotel
in 1906.

THE OLD JOLLY SMOKERS
Once at 25 The Mayorhold
Northampton

This inn once stood in the old part of town but was demolished post-war to make way for a hotel. The name speaks for itself.

This inn is said to have been haunted by a cowled figure and the smell of incense. It is believed that a maze of subterranean tunnels existed at one time, supposedly dug by the monks to link two of their monasteries. This would certainly explain the hauntings.

The Old Jolly Smokers when a café in 1963.

THE UNICORN INN [now demolished]
Rushden

Not only was the powdered horn of a unicorn believed to be an aphrodisiac but it was also thought that dipping the horn in a suspicious liquid would determine whether or not it contained any poison. These beliefs led to it being the sign for chemists and apothecaries ... not an auspicious sign for an inn.

The publican, interviewed in 1996, spoke of light switches going on and off while chills and waves of heat could be felt, following one another in quick succession. He told of hearing the sounds of beer being delivered into the cellar and the sound of movement and footsteps in empty rooms. The response given to me by an elderly gentleman living nearby was, "Well, that's no surprise. There used to be a mortuary out the back of the pub, was there for years."

THE GREEN MAN
Brackley Hatch
Syresham

The Green Man is said to be the sign of 'green life over winter and death'. Also known as Jack of the Woods and The Old Man of the Woods, there is possibly a connection to the old forests which at one time covered most of Northamptonshire.

In the early 18th century, those two infamous outlaws Dick Turpin and Jack Sheppard spread fear and terror in south Northamptonshire. Whittlebury Forest was a favourite haunt of theirs, where they would lie in wait for travellers on the road between Oxford and Peterborough. *The Green Man* became the headquarters for the Bow Street Runners while they were hunting for the highwaymen.

Unfortunately, with the passing of time and the passing of landlords at this ancient inn, any old tales would appear to have been long forgotten.

THE EXETER ARMS [now a private house]
Wakerley

The inn took its name from the Marquess of Exeter whose family, the Cecils, once lived in the Manor House which was demolished in about 1760. In the church, and spanning over 200 years, can be found the graves of the Exeter family.

The inn had several ghosts, one of whom was a young girl pining for the lover who had jilted her for someone else. Apparently the past landlord was in possession of a photograph of a ghost plus a wealth of spooky tales which, sadly, will now never be told over the bar on a winter's night.